Becoming

Transcendence: A Journey of Awakening and Transformation

Tony Reyna, M.A.

Becoming

To my parents, who have always supported me in my pursuit of knowledge and personal growth. Your love and encouragement have been the foundation upon which I have built my life and career. Thank you for instilling in me a passion for learning and a deep appreciation for the power of the human mind. This book is dedicated to you with love and gratitude.

I would also like to dedicate this book to my life partner, Scyler Gransbury. Your encouragement has been invaluable throughout my journey as a scholar and writer. You gave me the support I needed to be a true leader and an inspiration to others. I am honored to have you in my life and to dedicate this book to you.

Finally, I dedicate this book to all those who are seeking to awaken their consciousness and transform their lives. May it serve as a source of inspiration, guidance, and support on your journey of self-discovery and personal growth.

CONTENTS

Introduction: Awakening Consciousness

Awakening consciousness refers to expanding our awareness and understanding of ourselves, others, and the world. It involves becoming more conscious of our thoughts, feelings, and behaviors, as well as the interconnectedness of all things. Awakening consciousness is a continuous journey that leads to greater wisdom, compassion, and personal growth.

In this chapter, we will explore the concept of awakening consciousness, including its definition, importance, and practical ways to cultivate it.

What is Awakening Consciousness?

Awakening consciousness involves becoming more conscious of our inner and outer experiences. It means becoming more aware of our thoughts, emotions, and behaviors, as well as the impact they have on ourselves and others. It also involves developing a deeper understanding of the interconnectedness of all things and recognizing that we are all part of a larger whole.

This process takes many forms and can be experienced in various ways. Some people may have a sudden realization or epiphany that shifts their perspective and changes the way they view their reality. Others may gradually become more conscious through practices such as meditation, yoga, or mindfulness. Regardless of the method, the goal of awakening consciousness is to expand our awareness and understanding of ourselves and our life.

Why is Awakening Consciousness Important?

There are many reasons awakening consciousness is important. Here are just a few:

Personal Growth: Awakening consciousness can help us grow and develop as individuals. By becoming more aware of our thoughts, emotions, and behaviors, we can identify patterns that may hold us back and work to overcome them. We can also develop greater self-awareness and self-compassion, which can improve our relationships with ourselves and others.

Improved Relationships: Awakening consciousness can also improve our relationships with others. By developing greater empathy and compassion, we can better understand and connect with the people in our lives. We can also become more aware of how our actions and words impact others and work to communicate more effectively.

Greater Wisdom: Awakening consciousness can lead to greater wisdom and understanding of life. By recognizing the interconnectedness of all things, we can develop a deeper appreciation for the complexity and beauty of our world. We can also become more open-minded and accepting of different perspectives and ideas.

Positive Impact: Finally, awakening consciousness can have a positive impact on the world. By becoming more conscious of our actions and the impact they have on others, we can work to create positive change in our communities and beyond.

How to Cultivate Awakening Consciousness?

There are many ways to cultivate awakening consciousness. Here are some practical tips to get started:

- Practice mindfulness: Mindfulness is the practice of being present and fully engaged in the current moment. It involves paying attention to our thoughts, emotions, and physical sensations without judgment. Mindfulness can help us become more aware of our inner experiences and develop greater self-awareness. It can also help us develop greater empathy and compassion for others.

- Reflect on your values: Reflecting on our values can help us develop greater clarity and direction in our lives. Take some time to consider what is most important to you and how you want to design your life. This can help you develop a sense of purpose and meaning.

- Seek out new experiences: Trying new things can help us expand our horizons and develop new perspectives. Consider trying a new hobby, traveling to a new place, or meeting new people. This can help you break out of old patterns and develop greater awareness of the world around you.

- Read and learn: Reading and learning can help us develop greater knowledge and understanding of the world. Consider reading books on topics that interest you or taking courses on new subjects. This can help you develop greater wisdom and perspective.

- Engage in self-reflection: Regular reflection on self is simply asking yourself deep, reflective questions can help you to gain insight into your inner workings. Questions like "What are my core values?" or "What am I most afraid of?" can help you to identify areas for growth and self-improvement.

Remember, self-reflection is a practice that takes time and patience. It requires a willingness to look honestly at yourself and to be open to change. But by engaging in self-reflection regularly, you can gain greater self-awareness, insight, and personal growth. I will discuss more of these tips in depth.

Self-Reflection

Self-reflection is an essential tool in the journey towards awakening consciousness. It is a process of examining and understanding one's own thoughts, feelings, and actions to gain greater insight into ourselves. By engaging in self-reflection, individuals can gain a deeper understanding of their beliefs, values, and behaviors, and develop greater self-awareness.

At its core, self-reflection is about taking the time to pause and reflect on one's experiences, thoughts, and emotions. This can be done in a variety of ways, such as through journaling, meditation, or simply taking a few minutes to sit quietly and reflect. Regardless of your method that works best for you, the key is to be present in the moment and open to whatever thoughts and emotions arise and being honest with yourself.

Through self-reflection, individuals can begin to recognize patterns in their thoughts, feelings, and behaviors. This process will help you identify areas where you may be stuck or struggling and you will begin to develop new ways of thinking and behaving that are more aligned with your values and goals. It can also help individuals develop greater empathy and understanding towards others, as they become more aware of their own biases and assumptions.

In addition to promoting greater self-awareness and empathy, self-reflection also helps individuals develop a deeper sense of purpose and meaning in their lives. By reflecting on their values and goals, individuals can gain clarity on what is truly important to them and begin to take steps towards living a more fulfilling and meaningful experience of life.

Furthermore, self-reflection is a powerful tool that can help individuals develop greater resilience in the face of challenges and setbacks. By taking the time to reflect on their experiences and emotions, individuals can gain a greater sense of perspective and learn from their mistakes. This can help them bounce back from setbacks more quickly and effectively, and ultimately, lead to greater personal growth and development.

What is the difference between Conscious Awareness and Non-Conscious?

Conscious awareness and nonconsciousness are two states of consciousness that have been extensively studied by psychologists, neuroscientists, and philosophers. These two states are vastly different, and understanding their differences is critical to understanding human behavior, perception, and experience.

Conscious awareness is a state of awreness to one's surroundings, thoughts, and feelings. It is the state of being present and engaged with the environment. It is a subjective experience that can be described as a sense of self-awareness. Conscious awareness is typically associated with the brain's prefrontal cortex, which is responsible for decision-making, attention, and planning. In this state, the individual is fully aware of their thoughts and actions, and they can choose to engage or disengage with stimuli. Conscious awareness is what we typically think of as "being awake" and "being alert."

Nonconsciousness is also a state of being but being unaware of one's surroundings, thoughts, and feelings. It is the state of being disconnected from the environment. Nonconsciousness is also referred to as the unconscious mind, and it is associated with the brain's basal ganglia, which is responsible for controlling movement and basic physiological processes. In this state, the individual is not aware of their thoughts or actions, and they are not able to choose to engage or disengage with stimuli. Nonconsciousness is what we typically think of as "being asleep" or "being in a coma."

The main difference between conscious awareness and nonconsciousness is the level of awareness and control. Another difference between conscious awareness and nonconsciousness is the level of processing. In conscious awareness, information is processed at a high level of complexity and is integrated with prior knowledge, emotions, and motivations. In nonconsciousness, information is processed at a lower level of complexity and is not integrated with prior knowledge, emotions, or motivations. Nonconscious processes are automatic and do not require conscious attention or effort.

There are several theories about the relationship between conscious awareness and nonconsciousness. Some theories suggest that conscious awareness is an emergent property of nonconscious processes. According to these theories, conscious awareness arises when nonconscious processes reach a certain level of complexity. Other theories suggest that conscious awareness and nonconsciousness are two independent processes that interact with each other. According to these theories, conscious awareness can influence nonconscious processes, and nonconscious processes can influence conscious awareness. Understanding the differences between these two states is essential to understanding human behavior, perception, and experience.

Awakening Consciousness in Eastern Philosophies

In Eastern philosophy, the concept of awakening consciousness is a central idea that many spiritual traditions have explored, including Hinduism, Buddhism, Taoism, and Zen. At its core, awakening consciousness refers to a profound shift in awareness that allows individuals to transcend the limitations of the ego and connect with the deeper truths of the universe.

The ego, in Eastern philosophy, is seen as the source of all suffering. It is the part of us that is focused on the individual self, driven by desires, fears, and attachments. When we identify with the ego, we cannot see beyond our limited perceptions of ourselves and the world. This leads to a sense of separation, isolation, and dissatisfaction.

Awakening consciousness involves shifting awareness from the ego to the true self, which is often referred to as the Atman or the Tao. They facilitate this shift through spiritual practices such as meditation, yoga, and self-inquiry, which help to quiet the mind and cultivate greater awareness and presence.

Through transformation of awakened consciousness, we can connect with the deeper truths of the universe, which are often described as universal consciousness or cosmic consciousness. This is the realization that everything in the universe is interconnected, and that the individual self is just a small part of a greater whole.

The importance of awakening consciousness in Eastern philosophy lies because it leads to greater inner peace, happiness, and fulfillment. By transcending the limitations of the ego and connecting with the deeper truths of the universe, we can experience a sense of unity and oneness that is beyond words. This leads to a sense of freedom from the suffering caused by the ego, and a greater sense of connection with all beings.

In addition, we see awakening consciousness in Eastern philosophy to contribute to the greater good of society. By awakening to our true nature and connecting with the deeper truths of the universe, we can live in greater harmony with others and with the natural world. This leads to a more compassionate, empathetic, and sustainable world.

We can understand awakening consciousness through a variety of practices and traditions. In Hinduism, for example, they often describe awakening consciousness as the realization of the true self, which is said to be identical to Brahman, the ultimate reality of the universe. They achieved this realization through practices such as yoga, meditation, and self-inquiry, which help to quiet the mind and reveal the true nature of the self.

In Buddhism, they often refer awakening consciousness to as enlightenment or nirvana. This is the realization of the true nature of reality, which is characterized by impermanence, suffering, and non-self. We achieve this realization through practices such as meditation, mindfulness, and the study of Buddhist teachings.

In Taoism, awakening consciousness refers to as the realization of the Tao, which is the underlying principle of the universe. Realization is achieved through practices such as meditation, martial arts, and the cultivation of inner stillness.

In Zen, they often describe awakening consciousness as the realization of the true nature of the self, which is characterized by emptiness and interdependence. We achieve this realization through practices such as meditation, mindfulness, and the study of Zen teachings.

Regardless of the specific tradition or practice, the goal of awakening consciousness is the same: to transcend the limitations of the ego and connect with the deeper truths of the universe. This process can be challenging, as it requires us to confront our deepest fears, desires, and attachments. However, the rewards of awakening consciousness are immense, as they lead to greater inner peace, happiness, and fulfillment, and contribute to the transformation of oneness.

2

The Illusion of Separation: An Exploration of Oneness

In our everyday lives, we often experience a sense of separation from the world around us. We see ourselves as distinct and separate individuals, with our own thoughts, feelings, and experiences. This sense of separation can be so strong that we may feel isolated and disconnected from others, even as we interact with them. However, many spiritual traditions teach that this sense of separation is an illusion, and that we are all connected at a deeper level of reality. In this chapter, we will explore the illusion of separation and its implications for our understanding of consciousness and the world.

The Roots of Separation

The sense of separation that we experience in our lives is deeply ingrained in our culture and our way of thinking. From a young age, we are taught to see ourselves as individuals with our own unique identities and personalities. We are taught to value independence and self-reliance, and to see ourselves as separate from others. This sense of separation is reinforced by our society and the structures of power and control that shape our lives.

The roots of this separation can be traced back to the rise of modernity and the enlightenment, which emphasized reason, individualism, and the pursuit of knowledge and progress. This worldview encouraged people to see themselves as separate from nature and from each other, and to believe in the power of science and technology to control and shape the world.

The Illusion of Separation

Despite the strong cultural and social forces that reinforce the sense of separation, many spiritual traditions teach that this separation is an illusion. These traditions argue that we are all interconnected at a deeper level of reality, and that the boundaries between individuals are not as fixed as we might think. One of the most famous expressions of this idea is found in the Hindu concept of Advaita, which means "not-two" or "non-duality." According to this philosophy, the world is not composed of separate, individual entities, but rather is a seamless web of interdependent phenomena. The individual self, or ego, is seen as an illusion, a temporary manifestation of the underlying unity of all things.

This idea is echoed in many other spiritual traditions, including Buddhism, Taoism, and Sufism. In each of these traditions, the illusion of separation is seen as a fundamental error of perception, a misunderstanding of the nature of reality.

Implications for Consciousness

The idea that we are all interconnected at a deeper level of reality has profound implications for our understanding of consciousness. If the boundaries between individuals are not as fixed as we might think, then it becomes more difficult to define what we mean by "individual consciousness." Some spiritual traditions argue that consciousness is not an individual phenomenon, but rather a universal field of awareness that permeates all of existence. According to this view, we are all expressions of this universal consciousness, and our individual experiences are simply different perspectives on the same underlying reality. This view is echoed in the emerging field of consciousness studies, which is exploring the nature of consciousness from a scientific perspective. Researchers in this field are beginning to question the assumption that consciousness is solely a product of the brain and are exploring the possibility that consciousness may be a fundamental aspect of the universe itself.

Implications for the World

The idea that we are all interconnected at a deeper level of reality also has profound implications for our understanding of the world around us. If we are all part of a larger whole, then our actions and choices have ripple effects that extend far beyond our individual lives.

This idea is reflected in the concept of karma, which is central to many spiritual traditions. According to this idea, our actions have consequences not only for ourselves, but for everyone around us. By recognizing our interconnectedness, we can begin to take responsibility for our actions and work towards creating a more harmonious and compassionate life.

In addition, the illusion of separation can lead to a sense of alienation and disconnection from the natural world. If we see ourselves as separate from nature, we may be more likely to exploit and damage the environment, rather than seeing ourselves as part of a larger ecological system. By recognizing our interconnectedness with nature, we can begin to cultivate a deeper sense of respect and care for our environment.

Overcoming the Illusion of Separation

The illusion of separation is deeply ingrained in our culture and our way of thinking and overcoming it can be a difficult and ongoing process. However, there are several practices and approaches that can help us cultivate a deeper sense of connection and oneness with the world.

One approach is through meditation and mindfulness practices, which can help us become more aware of the ways in which our thoughts and perceptions shape our experiences. By learning to observe our thoughts without judgment, we can begin to see the ways in which our sense of self is constructed and maintained.

Another approach is through cultivating empathy and compassion for others. By recognizing the interconnectedness of all beings, we can begin to see the suffering of others as our own suffering, and work towards creating a more just and equitable world.

Finally, we can work towards breaking down the social and cultural structures that reinforce the illusion of separation. This may involve challenging the values of individualism and competition that are so deeply ingrained in our society and working towards creating more collaborative and community-based models of living. The illusion of separation is a powerful force in our lives, shaping the way we see ourselves and our place in the world. However, many spiritual traditions and emerging scientific fields are pointing towards a deeper truth: that we are all interconnected at a fundamental level of reality.

It is through the recognition of our fundamental unity that we can awaken to a new level of consciousness, one that sees the world in a new light and opens new possibilities for growth and transformation. As we awaken to the illusion of separation, we may begin to see the world in a new way. We may start to question the assumptions and beliefs that have shaped our lives and become more open to new ideas and perspectives. We may begin to see the world as a complex and interconnected web of relationships, rather than a collection of isolated individuals.

This shift in perspective can be both liberating and challenging. On the one hand, it can open new possibilities for growth and transformation, allowing us to see the world in a more holistic and integrated way. On the other hand, it can be difficult to reconcile this new way of seeing with the cultural and social structures that reinforce the illusion of separation. One of the key challenges in overcoming the illusion of separation is learning to navigate the tension between our individual identity and our sense of interconnectedness. While recognizing our interconnectedness can be liberating, it can also be disorienting, as we may feel like we are losing our sense of self. However, it is important to remember that our individual identity is not erased by recognizing our interconnectedness; rather, it is enriched by it. Another challenge is learning to navigate the complexity of our interconnected world. As we recognize our interconnectedness, we may become more aware of the ways in which our actions impact others and our environment. This can be overwhelming at times, as we may feel powerless to make a difference. However, by working towards small changes in our own lives, we can begin to create ripples of positive change that extend far beyond ourselves.

Ultimately, the awakening to the illusion of separation is a process of growth and transformation that requires both inner work and outer action. It requires us to question the assumptions and beliefs that have shaped our lives, and to work towards creating a more just and fairer world. It requires us to cultivate empathy and compassion for others, and to recognize the interconnectedness of everything that is living.

As we continue to awaken to the illusion of separation, we may see the world with different eyes. We may recognize the beauty and interconnectedness of all things, and to work towards creating a more fulfilling life of compassion and empathy. It is through awakening that we can cultivate a deeper sense of meaning and purpose in our lives and contribute to the blossoming of all beings.

The illusion of separation can also manifest in the way we approach conflict and difference. When we see ourselves as separate from others, we may be more likely to view differences as threats or obstacles to be overcome, rather than opportunities for growth and learning. We may become defensive or aggressive when our beliefs are challenged, rather than engaging in dialogue and seeking to understand different perspectives.

However, when we recognize our interconnectedness, we may approach conflict and difference differently. We may see these situations as opportunities for growth and learning, rather than threats to our identity. We may approach them with curiosity and openness, seeking to understand the perspectives of others and to find common ground. This approach to conflict can be transformative, both in our personal relationships and in the larger social and political spheres. It can help us move beyond the divisive rhetoric that so often characterizes our public discourse and to work towards creating more collaborative and inclusive models of decision-making.

The awakening to the illusion of separation is deepening our awareness and expanding our sense of identity. It requires us to recognize how we are interconnected with all beings, and to work towards creating equality in our world. It requires us to cultivate empathy and compassion for others, and to approach conflict and difference with curiosity and openness. As we continue this path of awakening, we may experience moments of profound insight and clarity, as well as moments of doubt and uncertainty. However, by staying committed to the process of growth and transformation, we can continue to expand our awareness and deepen our sense of connection with the world.

The illusion of separation is a powerful force in our lives, shaping the way we see ourselves and our reality. However, as we awaken to our interconnectedness, we can break free from this illusion and cultivate a deeper sense of meaning and purpose in our reality. By recognizing our interconnectedness, we can overcome the sense of alienation and disconnection that is so prevalent in our culture, and work towards creating a more harmonious and compassionate life. It is through the recognition of our fundamental unity that we can awaken to a new level of consciousness, one that sees the world in a new light and opens new possibilities for growth and transformation.

We may experience moments of struggle and doubt, but we can take comfort knowing that we are part of a larger web of relationships, and that our actions can have a positive impact on the world. By staying committed to the process of growth and transformation, we can continue to expand our awareness and deepen our sense of connection with the universe.

Illusion of Separation and Nature

The illusion of separation also affects our relationship with nature. When we see ourselves separate from nature, we may view it as a resource to be exploited, rather than as a living system in which we are a part. We may fail to recognize the interdependence of all living beings, and the impact that our actions have on the health and wellbeing of the planet. However, as we awaken to the illusion of separation, we can foster a deeper connection with nature. We may see the natural world as a source of inspiration and wonder, rather than simply as a resource to be abuse. We may recognize the intrinsic value of all living beings, and work towards creating a more sustainable and regenerative relationship with the planet. This shift in perspective can be transformative, both for our personal wellbeing and for the health of the planet. By recognizing our interconnectedness with nature, we may become more attuned to the natural rhythms and cycles of life, and more respectful of the fragile balance of our ecosystems.

We may also take action to address the environmental challenges that we face, such as climate change and habitat destruction. By recognizing the impact that our actions have on the planet, we may become more motivated to change our own lives, and to advocate for broader systemic change. Ultimately, the awakening to the illusion of separation is a call to action. It requires us to recognize the connection of all beings, and to work towards equivalence in our globe. It requires us to encourage empathy and compassion for others, and to approach conflict and difference with curiosity and openness. And it requires us to take responsibility for our impact on the planet, and to work towards creating a more sustainable and regenerative relationship with nature.

Continuing this path of awakening, we may encounter challenges and setbacks, but we can take comfort knowing that we are part of a larger web of relationships, and that our actions can have a positive impact on the world. By staying committed to the process of growth and transformation, we can continue to expand our awareness and deepen our sense of relation with the Earth and contribute to the thriving of all beings. By awakening to our interconnectedness, we can begin to break free from this illusion and cultivate a deeper sense of meaning and purpose in our lives.

3

The Power of Awareness

Have you ever stopped to truly observe your thoughts and feelings, and how they shape your experience of the world? The power of awareness lies in its ability to help us see beyond the surface level of our thoughts and emotions, and to promote a deeper understanding of ourselves and our surroundings. When we become aware of our thoughts and feelings, we can begin to identify patterns and tendencies that may be holding us back or causing us suffering. For example, we may notice a recurring negative thought pattern that undermines our confidence, or a habitual reaction to stress that causes us to lash out at others.

Through awareness, we can begin to untangle these patterns and develop new, more positive ways of thinking and reacting. We can learn to observe our thoughts and emotions without judgment, and to respond to them with compassion and self-care. This process of self-awareness and self-reflection is essential to personal growth and transformation. Awareness also has the power to transform our relationship with the natural world. When we become more aware of our surroundings, we can begin to see the beauty and complexity of the physical universe, and to appreciate the connection of all things.

Within awareness, we may begin to recognize the impact that our actions have on the planet, and to take steps to reduce our environmental footprint. We may become more attuned to the needs and feelings of others and develop greater empathy and compassion. Ultimately, awareness has the power to shift our consciousness, and to open us up to new levels of understanding and insight. Through the practice of mindfulness and meditation, we can learn to quiet our minds and connect with a deeper sense of inner peace and stillness.

In this state of expanded awareness, we may begin to glimpse a transcendent reality beyond our everyday experience. We may begin to see the interconnectedness of all things, and to feel a sense of oneness with the universe. This experience of transcendence can be transformative, leading to a profound shift in our understanding of ourselves and our environment. We may begin to see our lives as part of a larger cosmic story, and to feel a sense of purpose and meaning that transcends our individual concerns. However, it's important to note that the journey towards transcendence is not always easy. It requires a willingness to confront our deepest fears and insecurities, and to let go of old patterns and beliefs that may be holding us back. It also requires a commitment to ongoing self-reflection and self-awareness, as we continue to explore the depths of our consciousness and connect with the transcendent reality beyond our everyday experience.

Despite these challenges, the rewards of this journey are immense. Through the power of awareness, we can tap into a deeper sense of purpose and meaning and begin to live more fully and authentically. We can encourage greater responsiveness and compassion for others, and work towards creating a more balanced and impartial world. In this way, the journey towards transcendence is not just an individual journey, but a collective one. As we awaken to our interrelation and work towards a shared vision of a better world, we can create a more beautiful and empathetic world for all beings.

The power of awareness lies in its ability to help us see beyond the surface level of our thoughts and emotions, and to connect with a deeper sense of purpose and meaning. Through the practice of mindfulness and meditation, we can promote a greater sense of self-awareness and self-reflection and begin to tap into a transcendent reality beyond our everyday experience. This journey towards transcendence is not always comfortable, but the rewards are immense, both for us and for the external world.

As we continue this journey of awareness and transcendence, it's important to remember that there is no one-size-fits-all approach. Each of us has a unique path to follow, and our journeys may unfold in different ways and at different times. Some of us may find that mindfulness and meditation are powerful tools for cultivating awareness and connecting with the transcendent reality. Others may find that spending time in nature, engaging in creative pursuits, or practicing acts of service and compassion are the best ways to deepen their sense of awareness and purpose. Regardless of the path we choose, what is important is that we remain open and receptive to the guidance and insights that come our way. We must remain willing to let go of old beliefs and patterns that no longer serve us, and to embrace new ways of thinking and being that align with our highest aspirations.

It's also important to recognize that the journey towards transcendence is not a linear one. We may experience setbacks, challenges, and moments of doubt along the way. However, these moments can also be opportunities for growth, as we learn to face our fears and limitations with courage and resilience. Ultimately, the power of awareness lies in its ability to connect us with our truest selves, and with the external reality. Through awareness, we can support greater empathy, compassion, and understanding for ourselves and others, and work towards creating a more unbiased world.

So let us continue this journey of awakening and transformation with courage, compassion, and a deep sense of purpose. Let us embrace the power of awareness and open ourselves up to the transcendent reality that lies beyond our everyday experience. In doing so, we can create a brighter future, not just for ourselves, every being that are connected to this vast universe. The power of awareness is not just limited to our personal growth, but also has a profound impact on our relationships and interactions with others. When we become more aware of our thoughts, feelings, and behaviors, we are better able to recognize patterns of behavior that may harm our relationships and make conscious choices to change them.

Awareness also allows us to be more present and attentive to our interactions with others, which can improve the quality of our relationships and deepen our connections with those around us. By becoming more attuned to the needs and perspectives of others, we can foster greater understanding, and work towards creating a more harmonious and fulfilling relationships.

The power of awareness can extend beyond our immediate relationships and interactions, and into the wider world. When we become more aware of the interconnectedness of all things, we see how our actions and choices impact everything especially our responsiveness to our reality.

Through this heightened awareness, we can make more conscious and ethical choices in our consumption, our relationships, and our engagement with the world, contributing to a more sustainable way of living. The power of awareness is the power to transform in the better version of us. By becoming more aware of our thoughts, feelings, and behaviors, and by enriching a deeper sense of connection with the transcendent reality that lies beyond our everyday experience, we can work towards creating a happy and joyous reality.

So let us incorporate the power of awareness on our journey towards transcendence, and let it guide us towards a more fulfilling and purposeful life, one that is rooted in empathy, compassion, and connection. As a student of psychology, I realize the immense potential that lies in the power of awareness. Through my studies and personal experiences, I have witnessed how enlightening awareness can be. A powerful tool for not only personal growth but also for catalyzing social and collective change. At its core, awareness refers to the ability to pay attention to and observe one's thoughts, feelings, and behaviors without judgment or attachment. This ability to step back and observe oneself with a sense of curiosity and openness can lead to a greater understanding of oneself.

In recent years, there has been an increasing interest in the role of awareness in psychological wellbeing and personal growth. Research has shown that cultivating awareness through practices such as mindfulness meditation can lead to reductions in stress, anxiety, and depression, as well as improvements in cognitive functioning and emotional regulation.

Awareness can also be a tool for empowering individuals to create internally or externally. By becoming more aware of their thoughts, feelings, and behaviors, individuals can identify patterns and habits that prevent them from achieving their goals or living a fulfilling life. With this awareness, they can then make conscious choices to change these patterns and cultivate new habits that align with their values and aspirations. However, the power of awareness extends far beyond the individual level. When individuals become more aware of their own biases, beliefs, and actions, they can see how these factors contribute to larger social and systemic issues. This awareness can be a facilitator for social change, as individuals become motivated to take action to address issues such as inequality, injustice, and environmental degradation.

Cultivating awareness can also foster a greater sense of empathy, compassion, and interconnectedness with others. When individuals become more aware of their own struggles and challenges, they can better understand and relate to the struggles of others. This sense of empathy and understanding can inspire individuals promote change. The power of awareness is a force that can be harnessed for both personal and collective change. By developing mindfulness, individuals can gain the ability to transform both their own lives and the world they live in. As individuals become more conscious of their thoughts, emotions, and actions, they can also cultivate a deeper sense of compassion and interconnectedness with those around them, which ultimately fosters a more equitable and benevolent society. As a student of psychology, I am convinced that heightened awareness has the potential to foster both individual development and societal transformation, and I am eagerly anticipating the ways in which this awareness will continue to shape our world in the future.

An essential advantage of developing awareness is the ability to be more mindful and engaged in our daily experiences. Many times, we navigate life automatically, permitting our thoughts and feelings to dictate our behavior and responses. Nevertheless, by enhancing our consciousness, we can detach ourselves and perceive our thoughts and emotions objectively, providing us with the freedom to decide how we wish to react to them. This can be useful in situations where we may have previously reacted impulsively or emotionally. For example, imagine a scenario where a co-worker makes a snide comment about your work. Without awareness, you may react defensively or angrily, leading to conflict and tension in the workplace.

However, with awareness, you may notice the initial feeling of defensiveness and choose to respond in a more thoughtful and composed way, perhaps by calmly addressing the issue with your co-worker.

Through the practice of mindfulness, individuals can start to assert greater authority over their lives, making deliberate choices in response to their environment. This can result in heightened levels of self-empowerment, self-assurance, and a greater ability to navigate challenging circumstances. Additionally, the cultivation of awareness can have far-reaching effects on our relationships with others. When we become more attentive and engaged in our interactions, we develop the ability to listen, understand and connect with those around us. Consequently, this can lead to more rewarding and profound relationships, fostering a greater sense of social belonging and connection.

The influence of mindfulness can extend to a broader spectrum, empowering individuals to drive social and environmental progress. By heightening our consciousness of how our conduct and choices affect our surroundings, we can adopt more sustainable and responsible practices to mitigate our impact on the planet. Additionally, by developing an awareness of social challenges like discrimination, poverty, and inequality, we can take concrete steps towards remedying these issues and advancing a more equitable and just society.

To summarize, the power of mindfulness is a catalyst for profound personal and societal transformation. By developing awareness, individuals can embody greater mindfulness, empathy, and presence in their interactions with themselves and others. Furthermore, they can assert greater agency in their lives, making intentional decisions in response to their environment. In my view, the power of awareness is a potent instrument that can be utilized to realize a more equitable, sustainable, and meaningful world for all.

4

Meditation and Mindfulness

"The present moment is the only moment available to us, and it is the door to all moments." - Thich Nhat Hanh

We spend most of our lives dwelling on the past or worrying about the future, often missing the beauty and potential of the present moment. Mindfulness and meditation are two powerful practices that can help us become more aware and present in our lives. These practices have been used for centuries to cultivate a deeper sense of awareness, inner peace, and self-realization.

Mindfulness

Mindfulness is the practice of being present and aware of the current moment without judgment. It involves paying attention to your thoughts, feelings, and surroundings in a non-reactive way. The goal of mindfulness is to develop a heightened sense of awareness, self-compassion, and acceptance. This can be practiced in various ways, including meditation, breathing exercises, and mindful movement. The most common form of mindfulness meditation involves sitting in a quiet space and focusing on your breath. You can also practice mindfulness while doing everyday activities such as eating, walking, or washing dishes.

The benefits of mindfulness are vast and include reducing stress, anxiety, and depression, improving emotional regulation and cognitive function, and enhancing overall well-being. This process can help you become more aware of your thoughts and emotions, allowing you to respond to them in a more constructive and positive way.

Meditation

Meditation is a mental practice that involves training your mind to focus and calm your thoughts. It has been practiced for thousands of years and is a core component of many spiritual and religious traditions. Meditation involves sitting in a quiet space, focusing on your breath or a specific object, and observing your thoughts without judgment. There are many types of meditation, including mindfulness meditation, loving-kindness meditation, and transcendental meditation. Each type of meditation has its unique benefits, but the overarching goal is to achieve a state of deep relaxation and inner peace.

Meditation has been proven to reduce stress and anxiety, improve concentration and memory, enhance creativity and problem-solving skills, and increase self-awareness and self-realization. Regular meditation practice can lead to profound changes in the brain and nervous system, promoting increased well-being, and an awakened state of consciousness.

The Connection between Mindfulness and Meditation

Mindfulness and meditation are often used interchangeably, but they are not the same thing. Mindfulness is a state of being, while meditation is a practice used to promote mindfulness. Meditation can be used as a tool to develop mindfulness, but mindfulness can also be practiced without meditation. Both mindfulness and meditation require a similar mindset, one of openness, curiosity, and non-judgment. They encourage us to become more aware of our thoughts and emotions and to respond to them in a more constructive way. By developing a greater sense of mindfulness and meditation, we can awaken to our true nature and the interconnectedness of all things.

Tips for Practicing Mindfulness and Meditation

1. Start small: Begin with just a few minutes of mindfulness or meditation each day and escalate the time as you become more comfortable with the practice.
2. Create a routine: Set aside a specific time and space for your practice, so it becomes a habit.
3. Focus on your breath: Use your breath as a focal point for your meditation practice. This can help you become more present and focused.
4. Be kind to yourself: Remember, mindfulness and meditation are practices, not it is not perfect. Be patient and compassionate with yourself as you develop your practice.
5. Seek guidance: Consider joining a mindfulness or meditation group or working with a teacher to deepen your practice.

Mindfulness and meditation are effective methods for attaining present-moment awareness and developing a profound sense of consciousness. Integrating these practices into daily life can also help to amplify their benefits. Once you have established a consistent meditation routine, you can naturally incorporate mindfulness into your daily activities. However, it can be beneficial to intentionally cultivate mindfulness during routine tasks, allowing you to deepen your practice and enhance your ability to remain present.

One way to do this is to practice mindfulness while performing routine tasks, such as washing dishes or folding laundry. Rather than rushing through the task or letting your mind wander, bring your full attention to the sensations, sights, and sounds of the activity. Notice the temperature and texture of the water as you wash dishes, or the feel of the fabric as you fold laundry. Engage all your senses in the present moment and let go of any distracting thoughts. Another way to incorporate mindfulness into daily life is to take regular mindful breaks throughout the day. Set a timer for a few minutes and use that time to simply be present with your breath or body sensations. You could also try a short walking meditation, focusing on the movement of your feet and the sensations in your body as you walk slowly and mindfully.

Incorporating mindful communication into your daily practice is another vital element of mindfulness. When conversing with others, aim to be fully present and attentive. Listen with genuine interest and an open mind, abstaining from interrupting or passing judgment. If you observe any impulses arising, acknowledge them and allow them to dissipate, redirecting your attention to the person you are conversing with.

It's helpful to bring mindfulness to your technology use. Many of us spend a significant amount of time on our devices, but this can easily become a mindless habit that detracts from our overall well-being. Try setting boundaries around your technology use, such as turning off notifications or scheduling designated times for checking email or social media. When you are using technology, practice mindfulness by focusing on the task at hand and being aware of your posture, breathing, and overall state of mind. Mindfulness and meditation are powerful tools for awakening to a more conscious and fulfilling life. By cultivating present-moment awareness and developing a deeper understanding of our own minds, we can break free from habitual patterns of thought and behavior and connect more fully with ourselves and the world.

Establishing a regular meditation practice may present a challenge, but by embracing patience, inquisitiveness, and an eagerness to learn, anyone can reap the benefits of mindfulness. As you advance in your practice, bear in mind that meditation is not a one-size-fits-all approach, and discovering the techniques and methods that work best for you may take time.

In essence, the objective of mindfulness and meditation is not to eradicate stress or unease from our lives, but to learn how to approach them with greater skill and compassion. By cultivating mindfulness, we can develop increased resilience, discernment, and contentment, and unlock the full extent of our human potential.

Mindfulness and meditation offer us the opportunity to develop self-awareness and deepen our understanding of our inner workings. With consistent practice, we learn to observe our thoughts, emotions, and physical sensations without judgment, leading to an improved understanding of our patterns of behavior, triggers, and values. This newfound self-awareness empowers us to make better decisions, communicate more effectively, and navigate our relationships and the world with greater skill and ease. Moreover, mindfulness and meditation cultivate empathy and compassion for others. By attuning ourselves to our own inner experiences, we develop a heightened capacity to empathize with others. This helps foster more meaningful connections, greater understanding, and a sense of community.

Lastly, mindfulness and meditation can help us uncover a sense of purpose or meaning in our lives. As we deepen our awareness, compassion, and wisdom, we may begin to see our lives from a broader perspective. We may question our values, what truly matters to us, and how we want to impact the world. Everyone's journey towards awakened consciousness is unique, and while the practices that help us achieve it may differ, the benefits are clear. Mindfulness and meditation can help us cultivate greater awareness, compassion, and wisdom, leading to a more fulfilling existence that is in alignment with our deepest aspirations.

Types of Meditation

There are several types of meditation that can be incorporated into a mindfulness practice, each with their own unique benefits. Here are a few examples:

Breath awareness meditation: This is one of the most common forms of meditation and involves focusing on the sensation of the breath as it moves in and out of the body. By bringing attention to the breath, we can begin to quiet the mind and cultivate a sense of inner peace.

To practice breath awareness meditation, find a comfortable seated position and bring your attention to the sensation of the breath. You can focus on the rise and fall of your chest or the sensation of air moving in and out of your nostrils. When your mind begins to wander (as it inevitably will), simply bring your attention back to the breath.

Loving-kindness meditation: Also known as metta meditation, this practice involves cultivating feelings of love and kindness towards us and others. By practicing loving-kindness, we can increase our sense of connection and compassion.

To practice loving-kindness meditation, start by finding a comfortable seated position and recall someone you love. It could be a friend, family member, or even a pet. Visualize them in your mind and silently repeat the following phrases: "May you be happy, may you be healthy, may you be safe, may you live with ease." Repeat these phrases several times before moving on to another person and eventually extending the practice to include yourself and all beings.

Body scan meditation: This practice involves bringing attention to different parts of the body and noticing any sensations or areas of tension. By cultivating awareness of the body, we can become more grounded and present in the moment.

To practice a body scan meditation, find a comfortable position lying down or seated. Begin by bringing your attention to the top of your head and slowly scan down your body, noticing any sensations or areas of tension. As you become more aware of your body, you may find that tension begins to release, and a sense of relaxation takes over.

Walking meditation: This practice involves bringing mindfulness to the act of walking, noticing the sensations of each step and the environment around us. Walking meditation can be a great way to bring mindfulness into our daily lives.

To practice walking meditation, find a quiet place to walk where you won't be disturbed. Begin by standing still and bringing your attention to your feet. As you take your first step, focus on the sensation of your foot lifting off the ground, moving through the air, and landing back down. Repeat this process with each step, bringing attention to the movement of the body and the environment around you.

These are just a few examples of the many types of meditation that can be incorporated into a mindfulness practice. By experimenting with different techniques, we can find what works best for us and cultivate a deeper sense of presence and awareness in our daily lives.

5

The Ego and Self-Identity

As we delve deeper into the journey of awakening consciousness, we cannot ignore the role of the ego and self-identity. These concepts are crucial in understanding the human psyche and how it impacts our thoughts, emotions, and behaviors. In this chapter, we will explore the nature of the ego, its functions, and its relationship with self-identity.

The Nature of the Ego

We can define the ego as the part of our psyche that defines our sense of self, separating us from others, and giving us a sense of individuality. It is the aspect of our personality that mediates between our inner world and the external world, enabling us to adapt to changing circumstances. Sigmund Freud, the father of psychoanalysis, described the ego as the mediator between the id (our instinctual desires) and the superego (our moral and ethical standards). According to Freud, the ego balances these opposing forces and achieving a state of equilibrium. While the ego serves a vital function in our lives, it can also lead to various psychological problems. For example, when the ego becomes too rigid or inflated, we may become narcissistic, self-centered, or overly competitive. When the ego is weak, we may struggle with low self-esteem, anxiety, or depression.

Functions of the Ego

The ego performs several essential functions that enable us to navigate our everyday lives. These functions include:

1. Reality Testing: The ego helps us distinguish between reality and fantasy, enabling us to perceive the world accurately.
2. Defense Mechanisms: The ego employs various defense mechanisms, such as repression, denial, and projection, to protect us from anxiety, stress, and other uncomfortable emotions.
3. Problem-Solving: The ego finds solutions to problems and making decisions.
4. Self-Regulation: The ego helps us regulate our emotions, impulses, and behaviors, enabling us to adapt to changing circumstances.

Self-Identity

Self-identity is almost similar to the ego and can define our sense of who we are, both as individuals and as members of a group or community. Various factors, including genetics, upbringing, culture, and personal experiences, shape self-identity. One of the primary challenges of self-identity is finding a balance between individuality and social connection. While we all have a unique identity, we are also social beings who crave connection and belonging. Finding this balance can be challenging, and many people struggle with issues such as conformity, social pressure, and identity crises.

The Role of the Ego in Self-Identity

The ego plays a crucial role in shaping our self-identity. As we develop from infancy to adulthood, we form a sense of who we are based on our experiences, relationships, and cultural influences. The ego mediates this process, helping us integrate various aspects of ourselves into a cohesive whole. However, the ego can also distort our self-identity, leading us to identify too strongly with certain aspects of ourselves or others. For example, if we base our sense of self solely on our achievements or social status, we may become overly attached to these external factors, leading to anxiety, stress, or a sense of emptiness. The ego and self-identity are complex and multifaceted concepts that play a crucial role in shaping our thoughts, emotions, and behaviors. By understanding these concepts and their impact on our lives, we can gain greater self-awareness and insight into our own inner workings. Through practices such as meditation, mindfulness, and self-reflection, we can unravel the complexities of our ego and develop a more balanced, integrated sense of self-identity.

The ego is an integral part of the human psyche, but it can also be a source of distress and suffering. Sometimes, the ego can become over-inflated, leading to feelings of superiority or entitlement. In others, it can become diminished, leading to feelings of worthlessness or insecurity. One of the key challenges of awakening consciousness is learning to recognize and manage the ego in a healthy manner. This involves developing a sense of self-awareness and fostering a deeper understanding of one's own motivations and desires.

One useful tool for this process is introspection. By taking time to reflect on our thoughts, feelings, and behaviors, we can identify patterns and tendencies that may be driven by the ego. Through this process, we can gain insight into our own psychological makeup and make conscious choices that are aligned with our authentic selves. Another important aspect of managing the ego is developing a sense of humility. This involves recognizing that we are not perfect and that we are all subject to limitations and imperfections. By acknowledging our own flaws and weaknesses, we can become more compassionate and understanding towards others, and less likely to become defensive or reactive when our ego is challenged.

It's also important to cultivate a sense of self-acceptance. This involves embracing all aspects of ourselves, including our strengths and weaknesses, and recognizing that they are all part of who we are. By accepting ourselves fully, we can develop a greater sense of self-worth and self-esteem, which can help us navigate the challenges of life with greater resilience and grace.

Finally, developing a sense of detachment from the ego is also important. This involves recognizing that the ego is just one aspect of our identity and that there is a larger, more expansive sense of self that transcends the limitations of the ego. Through practices such as meditation, we can begin to access this deeper sense of self and cultivate a greater sense of inner peace and contentment.

Self-Identity

Self-identity is a complex and dynamic concept that is closely related to the ego. It refers to the way in which individuals understand and define themselves in relation to others and the world around them. Self-identity is often shaped by a variety of factors, including social, cultural, and environmental influences. In psychology, the concept of self-identity is closely related to the idea of self-concept. Self-concept refers to the set of beliefs and perceptions that individuals have about themselves. This includes their beliefs about their personality traits, abilities, values, and social roles. Self-identity is a more specific aspect of self-concept, referring to the way in which individuals define themselves in relation to others and their surroundings.

One important aspect of self-identity is the degree to which it is stable or fluid. Some individuals have a strong sense of self-identity that is consistent across different contexts and experiences, while others may have a more fluid sense of self that is more easily influenced by external factors.

Another important aspect of self-identity is the degree to which it is influenced by social and cultural factors. In many cultures, for example, individual identity is closely tied to family, community, and social status. In other cultures, individual identity may be more focused on personal achievement and self-expression. From a psychological perspective, understanding self-identity can be useful in several ways. For example, research has shown that individuals with a strong and stable sense of self-identity tend to have higher levels of psychological well-being and are more resilient in the face of adversity. Conversely, individuals with a more fluid or unstable sense of self-identity may be more vulnerable to anxiety, depression, and other mental health issues.

In addition, understanding self-identity can be useful in the context of therapy and personal growth. By exploring and clarifying their own sense of self-identity, individuals can gain greater insight into their own values, motivations, and life goals. This can help them to make more informed decisions and to navigate life's challenges with greater confidence and resilience. Overall, the concept of self-identity is a complex and dynamic one that is closely related to the ego. We can achieve a more gratifying and purposeful existence by delving into and comprehending our own self-identity, which leads to a better understanding of ourselves and the world we live in.

6

The Role of Emotions

As an expert in psychology, I believe emotions play a critical role in the awakening consciousness process for humans. Emotions are complex, multi-dimensional experiences that shape how we perceive and respond to our existence. They can influence our thoughts, behaviors, and relationships with others. When we become more conscious of our emotions, we can gain greater insight into ourselves and our place in the world.

The Role of Emotions in Awakening Consciousness

We often think emotions of as either positive or negative, but they are much more complex. We can divide emotions into three basic categories: pleasant, unpleasant, and neutral. Pleasant emotions are those that make us feel good, such as joy, happiness, and contentment. Unpleasant emotions are those that make us feel bad, such as anger, sadness, and fear. Neutral emotions are those that do not have a strong emotional charge, such as boredom or indifference.

Emotions play a crucial role in the awakening consciousness process because they provide us with important information about ourselves and our environment. When we experience an emotion, it is often because something in our environment has triggered a response within us. This response can be a physical, emotional, or cognitive reaction to the situation at hand. By becoming more conscious of our emotions, we can gain insight into what triggers us and how we respond to different situations. For example, if someone experiences anxiety in social situations, they may become more conscious of their emotions and explore what triggers their anxiety. Through this process, they may discover that their anxiety is related to a fear of rejection or a belief that they are not good enough. Once they become more conscious of these underlying beliefs, they can work to challenge and reframe them, which can lead to greater emotional resilience and self-awareness. Hypnotherapy is effective in reprogramming limited beliefs.

Emotions can also play a role in our relationships with others. When we become more conscious of our emotions, we can better understand how our emotions impact our interactions with others. For example, if someone frequently experiences anger in response to their partner's behavior, they may become more conscious of this emotion and work to explore the underlying causes of their anger. Through this process, they may discover that they relate their anger to a feeling of disrespect or a need for control. By becoming more conscious of these underlying emotions, they can work to communicate their needs more effectively and develop healthier relationships with others.

Practical Strategies for Cultivating Emotional Consciousness

There are several practical strategies that can cultivate emotional consciousness. Here are a few examples:

Mindfulness: Mindfulness involves paying attention to our thoughts, feelings, and sensations in the present moment without judgment. This can help us become more conscious of our emotions and develop greater emotional awareness.

Journaling: Journaling can be a powerful tool for exploring our emotions and gaining insight into ourselves. By writing about our emotions, we can gain clarity about what triggers them and how they impact our lives.

Therapy: Therapy can be a valuable resource for exploring our emotions and developing greater emotional consciousness. A therapist can help us explore our emotions in a safe and supportive environment and provide us with strategies for managing difficult emotions.

Self-Reflection: Regular self-reflection can help us become more conscious of our emotions and how they impact our lives. Reflecting on our emotions, both positive and negative, can help us gain insight into ourselves and our relationships with others.

Mindful Breathing: Taking a few minutes each day to practice mindful breathing can help us become more conscious of our emotions and develop greater emotional regulation. Mindful breathing involves focusing our attention on our breath and observing our thoughts and emotions without judgment.

As a life student of awakening consciousness, I believe that emotions are pivotal in this process for humans. By raising our awareness of our emotions, we can gain valuable insights into ourselves, our environment, and our relationships with others. Emotions can act as vital cues, indicating what triggers us, what we require, and how we can communicate more effectively with others. Furthermore, emotional consciousness can assist us in developing better emotional regulation and resilience. When we heighten our consciousness of our emotions, we can learn to manage them more effectively, resulting in a more adaptable response to challenging situations. This, in turn, can foster greater emotional stability and an increased sense of well-being. However, it is crucial to recognize that emotional consciousness is not synonymous with emotional perfection. Negative emotions are a natural part of the human experience, and we may feel overwhelmed or reactive in certain situations. Nonetheless, by raising our emotional consciousness, we can cultivate a more intentional and adaptive response to these emotions.

Developing emotional consciousness is a gradual process that requires both commitment and dedication. It involves nurturing self-awareness, approaching our emotions with a curious and empathetic mindset, and devising effective techniques for regulating our emotions. By engaging in this process, we can awaken to a heightened level of self-awareness and interconnectedness with our surroundings.

Regulating Emotions

Regulating emotions is an essential aspect of the awakening consciousness process. Emotions are an integral part of human experience, but they can also be overwhelming and difficult to manage. By learning to regulate our emotions, we can cultivate a sense of emotional balance and wellbeing, which can enhance our capacity for self-awareness, compassion, and personal growth. There are several ways in which people can regulate their emotions during the awakening consciousness process. One of the most effective methods is through mindfulness practices. Mindfulness is a technique that involves paying attention to the present moment in a non-judgmental way. This practice can help us become more aware of our emotions and develop greater control over them. Mindfulness-based practices such as meditation, deep breathing exercises, and yoga can be powerful tools for regulating emotions. Research has shown that these practices can help reduce symptoms of anxiety, depression, and stress, as well as increase positive emotions such as joy, happiness, and contentment. By regularly practicing mindfulness, we can develop greater emotional regulation skills and a more profound sense of inner calm and balance.

Another way humans can regulate their emotions is by developing healthy coping mechanisms. Coping mechanisms are strategies we use to manage stress and difficult emotions. Examples of healthy coping mechanisms include exercise, spending time in nature, engaging in creative activities, and spending time with supportive friends and family members. By engaging in these activities, we can reduce feelings of distress and cultivate a sense of inner peace and wellbeing.

Humans can also regulate their emotions by developing healthy communication skills. Effective communication is an essential aspect of managing emotions in relationships. By learning how to express ourselves clearly and effectively, we can reduce the likelihood of misunderstandings, conflicts, and emotional reactivity. Healthy communication skills include active listening, using "I" statements, and expressing empathy and compassion towards others. Humans can regulate their emotions by seeking support from mental health professionals. Therapy and counseling can be valuable resources for individuals who are struggling with difficult emotions or mental health concerns. These professionals can provide guidance, support, and practical tools for managing emotions and improving emotional regulation skills.

To sum up, mastering emotional regulation is a crucial element of the process of awakening consciousness. Humans can acquire emotional regulation abilities by practicing mindfulness, creating healthy coping mechanisms, refining their communication skills, and seeking assistance from mental health professionals. By doing so, individuals can foster a heightened sense of emotional equilibrium, well-being, and personal development.

Understanding the Power of Emotional Intelligence

Emotional intelligence is a critical factor in awakening consciousness. It refers to the ability to recognize, understand, and manage one's own emotions, as well as the emotions of others. Emotional intelligence is a complex and multifaceted construct, encompassing a range of different skills and abilities. These skills include self-awareness, self-regulation, motivation, empathy, and social skills. I will go more in detail in the next sections.

One of the key aspects of emotional intelligence is self-awareness. This involves being able to recognize and understand one's own emotions, as well as the impact that these emotions can have on thoughts, behaviors, and interactions with others. By developing greater self-awareness, individuals can begin to identify patterns in their emotional responses and gain insight into how these responses may be contributing to challenges or difficulties in their lives.

They can also begin to recognize the ways in which their emotions may be influencing their thoughts and perceptions, and work to develop a more balanced and grounded perspective.

Another important aspect of emotional intelligence is self-regulation. This involves the ability to manage and regulate one's own emotions in healthy and constructive ways. Individuals who are high in emotional intelligence can recognize when they are becoming overwhelmed or triggered and take steps to calm themselves and regain a sense of balance. This may involve techniques such as deep breathing, mindfulness meditation, or physical exercise.

Empathy is another key aspect of emotional intelligence. This involves the ability to recognize and understand the emotions and perspectives of others. By developing greater empathy, individuals can become more attuned to the needs and experiences of those around them and cultivate more meaningful and authentic relationships. They can also develop greater compassion and understanding for others, which can help to promote a sense of connectedness and belonging.

Social skills are also an important component of emotional intelligence. This involves the ability to navigate social situations with ease and confidence, communicate effectively with others, and build strong and meaningful relationships. Individuals who are high in emotional intelligence can communicate their thoughts and feelings clearly and effectively and are skilled at resolving conflicts and managing interpersonal dynamics.

Emotional intelligence is a critical factor in awakening consciousness. By developing greater self-awareness, self-regulation, empathy, and social skills, individuals can cultivate a deeper sense of connectedness and purpose in their lives. They can also become more attuned to the needs and experiences of others, and work to promote greater understanding, compassion, and harmony in their relationships and communities.

Empathy, Compassion, and the Heart-Centered Path to Consciousness

Empathy and compassion are two key qualities that can help us connect with others on a deeper level and support a heart-centered path to consciousness. Empathy refers to the ability to understand and share the feelings of others, while compassion involves feeling concern for the suffering of others and a desire to ease it. Together, these qualities can help us develop greater sensitivity to the needs and experiences of others, and to cultivate a deeper sense of connection and empathy with all living things.

One of the key benefits of cultivating empathy and compassion is that it can help us develop a greater sense of connection and purpose in our lives. When we can see the world from the perspective of others, we recognize the interconnectedness of all beings and the impact that our actions can have on our environment. This can lead us to feel a greater sense of responsibility and commitment to making a positive impact in the world, and to work towards creating a more compassionate and awakened world.

Another benefit of empathy and compassion is that it can help us develop greater resilience in the face of adversity. When we can connect with others on a deep level and develop a sense of shared humanity, we are better able to cope with the challenges and difficulties that we encounter in our journey. We are also more likely to reach out for support and to offer support to others in need, which can help to create a sense of community and belonging.

One of the key practices for enriching empathy and compassion is mindfulness meditation. This involves learning to cultivate a sense of presence and awareness in the present moment, and to develop a non-judgmental attitude towards our thoughts and feelings. By learning to cultivate a sense of mindfulness and awareness, we can develop greater sensitivity to the needs and experiences of others, and to cultivate a deeper sense of empathy and compassion.

To sum up, having empathy and compassion are crucial traits that can lead us towards a path of consciousness centered on the heart. We can enhance our understanding of others' emotions and experiences and foster a feeling of shared humanity, which can bring us a sense of connection and meaning in life. With the aid of mindfulness meditation and other practices that focus on the heart, we can deepen our sense of empathy and compassion and strive towards a society that is more compassionate and equitable for all individuals.

Embracing the Full Spectrum of Emotions for Spiritual Growth

Emotions are a fundamental part of the human experience, and embracing the full spectrum of emotions is essential for spiritual growth and transformation. While many spiritual traditions emphasize the importance of cultivating positive emotions such as love, joy, and compassion, it is equally important to acknowledge and work with the full range of emotions, including those that are uncomfortable or difficult.

One reason why it is important to embrace the full spectrum of emotions is that our emotions can serve as powerful teachers and guides on our spiritual journey. When we experience difficult emotions such as fear, anger, or sadness, we are often being called to look more deeply at our beliefs, values, and patterns of behavior. By acknowledging and working with these difficult emotions, we can gain valuable insights into our own inner landscape and begin to uncover the deeper sources of our pain and suffering.

Another reason why it is important to embrace the full spectrum of emotions is that doing so can help us to improve greater resilience and emotional intelligence. When we learn to work with our emotions in a skillful and compassionate way, we are better able to navigate the ups and downs of life with greater ease and grace. We become more attuned to our own needs and the needs of others, and we are better able to communicate our thoughts and feelings in a clear and effective way.

Mindfulness meditation is a fundamental technique for embracing a broad range of emotions. It involves developing an attitude of non-judgment and cultivating mindfulness or awareness of the present moment. By mindfully observing our thoughts and feelings with compassion and curiosity, we can gain insight into their roots and learn to skillfully work with them. This understanding of our emotions can help us address them constructively.

Another key practice for embracing the full spectrum of emotions is self-compassion. This involves learning to treat ourselves with the same kindness and understanding that we would offer to a dear friend. By learning to offer ourselves compassion and understanding, we can begin to develop greater acceptance and resilience in the face of difficult emotions, and to cultivate a deeper sense of connection and empathy with ourselves and others.

Mindfulness meditation is a fundamental technique for embracing a broad range of emotions. It involves developing an attitude of non-judgment and cultivating mindfulness or awareness of the present moment. By mindfully observing our thoughts and feelings with compassion and curiosity, we can gain insight into their roots and learn to skillfully work with them. This understanding of our emotions can help us address them constructively.

I firmly conclude that embracing a broad spectrum of emotions is a prerequisite for spiritual growth and transformation. Acknowledging and handling the entire range of emotions helps us gain valuable insights into our inner selves and uncover the deeper roots of our pain and suffering. With greater resilience and emotional intelligence, we can navigate life's fluctuations more gracefully. Through mindfulness meditation and self-compassion practices, we can develop curiosity and compassion towards the full range of emotions and effectively manage them in a skillful and constructive way.

Navigating the Complexities of Emotional Vulnerability in Awakening

Emotional vulnerability is a complex and nuanced aspect of awakening consciousness. It can be uncomfortable and challenging, but it is also a crucial part of the journey. Learning how to navigate the complexities of emotional vulnerability is an essential skill for anyone who is serious about deepening their spiritual practice.

One of the first things to understand about emotional vulnerability is that it is not a weakness. In fact, it takes a great deal of courage and strength to allow ourselves to be vulnerable and to fully feel our emotions. It is important to remember that vulnerability is a natural and necessary part of the human experience, and that it is through our vulnerabilities that we can truly connect with ourselves and others.

It is important to recognize that emotional vulnerability can be uncomfortable and challenging. It can be tempting to avoid or suppress our emotions, especially when they are painful. However, this only serves to reinforce our patterns of avoidance and disconnection. Instead, we need to learn how to lean into our emotions and to be present with them, even when they are uncomfortable.

To navigate the intricacies of emotional vulnerability, mindfulness is a beneficial approach. It involves developing complete present-moment awareness without any judgment or distraction. By practicing mindfulness, we can observe our emotions with greater clarity and respond to them in a compassionate and skillful manner. Self-compassion is another powerful tool for navigating emotional vulnerability. It involves treating ourselves with kindness, understanding, and acceptance, particularly during times of struggle or pain. By learning to practice self-compassion, we can create a supportive and safe space that encourages us to express our emotions genuinely and vulnerably.

It is also important to recognize that emotional vulnerability is not a linear process. It is not something that can be mastered or overcome straightforwardly. Instead, emotional vulnerability is an ongoing practice that requires patience, self-awareness, and self-compassion. There will be times when we feel more vulnerable than others, and times when our emotions are challenging to navigate. In these moments, it is important to be gentle and patient with ourselves, and to remember that vulnerability is an ongoing process.

To conclude, navigating the intricacies of emotional vulnerability plays a pivotal role in the awakening process. It demands courage, self-awareness, and self-compassion. By practicing mindfulness and self-compassion, we can develop the ability to deal with our emotions more skillfully and empathetically. We can also acknowledge that vulnerability is a continual process and by doing so, create a safe and supportive environment that enables us to wholeheartedly embrace the complete range of our emotions.

Healing Trauma for Greater Emotional Freedom in Consciousness

Trauma is a common and often misunderstood aspect of the human experience. It can leave deep scars on our psyche and can have a profound impact on our emotional well-being. However, with the right tools and support, it is possible to heal from trauma and to experience greater emotional freedom in our consciousness.

To begin the journey of healing from trauma, it is crucial to acknowledge its presence. Trauma can present itself in various ways, including physical, emotional, and psychological symptoms. It is essential to recognize the symptoms of trauma, such as anxiety, depression, insomnia, or flashbacks, to start the healing process.

Seeking the assistance of a trained mental health professional can be beneficial for identifying and processing the effects of trauma. Such professionals have experience in recognizing the symptoms of trauma and can provide effective treatment modalities. Mental health professionals can offer a safe space for individuals to share their experiences and emotions, and work towards managing the impact of trauma on their lives.

Through therapy, individuals can learn coping skills to manage their emotions and establish healthy ways of expressing their feelings. Additionally, therapy can provide a sense of empowerment and resilience to cope with traumatic events. With the guidance of a mental health professional, individuals can begin to rebuild their lives and create a brighter future for themselves.

Another important step in healing from trauma is to develop self-compassion. Trauma can often leave us feeling powerless, ashamed, and unworthy. By learning to offer ourselves self-compassion, we can begin to release the shame and self-judgment that often accompanies trauma. This can create a sense of safety and support that allows us to explore and process the effects of our trauma more fully.

One helpful tool for healing from trauma is somatic therapy. Somatic therapy is a body-based approach to healing trauma that focuses on releasing physical tension and stored emotions. By working with a trained somatic therapist, we can learn to identify and release the physical sensations associated with trauma. This can help to create a sense of safety and relaxation in the body, which can support the processing and release of stored emotions.

Mindfulness meditation is a valuable tool for individuals who are healing from trauma. It involves developing complete present-moment awareness without any judgment or distraction. By practicing mindfulness, individuals can observe their thoughts and emotions with greater clarity and respond to them more skillfully and empathetically.

Mindfulness can be especially beneficial when processing the effects of trauma. It enables individuals to be more present with their emotions and to deal with them in a compassionate manner. By cultivating mindfulness, individuals can gain a deeper understanding of their inner experience and learn to respond to their emotions in a healthy and constructive way. Through mindfulness meditation, individuals can develop greater resilience and emotional intelligence, which can help them navigate the challenges of healing from trauma with greater ease and grace.

Ultimately, the journey of healing from trauma is a unique and individual process. It can be challenging, uncomfortable, and even painful at times. However, with the right tools and support, it is possible to heal from trauma and to experience greater emotional freedom in our consciousness. By acknowledging the presence of trauma, cultivating self-compassion, and exploring body-based approaches to healing, we can begin to release the hold that trauma has on our emotional well-being. This can create a greater sense of freedom and possibility in our consciousness, allowing us to fully embrace the present moment with greater joy and ease.

It's crucial to understand that the process of healing from trauma is not a linear. Progress can be slow or inconsistent, and setbacks are common. It's easy to feel discouraged or frustrated during such times. However, it's essential to recognize that healing is a gradual process of growth and learning that unfolds over time, and it is not a destination in and of itself.

In addition to individual efforts towards healing, community and support play a crucial role in the process. Trauma can be isolating, and it's common to feel alone in our struggles. However, connecting with others who have experienced similar trauma can create a sense of belonging and support that is immensely therapeutic. This can take many forms, such as support groups, individual therapy, or simply talking to trusted friends and family members who are willing to listen without judgment. By building a community of support, individuals can develop greater resilience and find the strength to continue their healing journey.

To conclude, it's crucial to recognize that the process of healing from trauma is different for everyone. It's natural to feel discouraged or frustrated when the progress seems slow or stagnant. However, it's important to keep in mind that healing is a journey, not a destination. It's a process of growth and learning that occurs gradually, with ups and downs along the way.

Furthermore, community and support play a vital role in healing from trauma. Since trauma can make one feel isolated, connecting with others who have experienced similar experiences can create a sense of community and support that can aid in healing. It could take various forms such as support groups, individual therapy, or merely talking with trusted friends and loved ones without judgment.

Lastly, it's critical to recognize that the process of healing from trauma is not only about releasing negative emotions and experiences. It's also about cultivating a sense of connection, joy, and purpose in life. As we heal from trauma, we may discover new interests, passions, or a greater capacity for empathy, compassion, and creativity. By embracing the full spectrum of emotions, we can create a life that is more vibrant, meaningful, and authentic. This journey of healing and transformation can lead to a deeper sense of consciousness and possibility, grounded in resilience, growth, and authenticity.

7

Spiritual Practices

Spiritual practices have been a part of human culture for thousands of years and have been used to cultivate a deeper connection to the divine, to oneself, and to others. In recent years, these practices have gained increased attention in psychology, as researchers and clinicians have recognized their potential for promoting well-being and personal growth. In this chapter, we will explore what spiritual practices are, why they are important for awakening consciousness, and the different spiritual practices that will be covered.

What are Spiritual Practices?

Spiritual practices are activities or rituals that facilitate spiritual growth and connection. They are often associated with religious or philosophical traditions but can also be practiced independently. Some examples of spiritual practices include meditation, prayer, yoga, mindfulness, breathwork, rituals and ceremonies, creative expression, and service to others. They typically aim these practices at developing greater awareness, compassion, and a sense of connection to something greater than oneself.

Why are Spiritual Practices Important for Awakening Consciousness?

Spiritual practices are important for awakening consciousness because they can help us cultivate a deeper sense of awareness and understanding of ourselves and the world. By engaging in these practices, we can develop greater insight into our thoughts, emotions, and behaviors, and learn to respond to them in more skillful and compassionate ways. This increased awareness can also help us become more attuned to the needs of others and to develop greater empathy and compassion.

By engaging in spiritual practices, we can foster a deeper connection with a force or entity beyond our individual selves. This connection can manifest in various ways, such as a bond with the natural world, a belief in a higher power, or a sense of purpose or significance in our existence. By strengthening this connection, we can enhance our ability to bounce back from difficult situations and find more purpose and satisfaction in our daily lives.

Types of Spiritual Practices:

There are many spiritual practices, each with their own unique benefits and challenges. Some practices in this chapter include:

1. Meditation: Meditation is a practice of focusing the mind and developing greater awareness of one's thoughts and emotions. There are many meditations, including mindfulness meditation, loving-kindness meditation, and mantra meditation.

2. Yoga: Yoga is a practice that combines physical postures, breathing techniques, and meditation to promote physical and spiritual well-being. There are many styles of yoga, each with their own unique focus and benefits.

3. Mindfulness: Mindfulness is a practice of developing greater awareness of one's thoughts, emotions, and bodily sensations in the present moment. It is often practiced through

meditation but can also be applied to daily activities such as eating, walking, or working.

4. Breathwork: Breathwork is a practice of using specific breathing techniques to promote physical and emotional well-being. It can help to reduce stress, anxiety, and depression, and promote a greater sense of relaxation and well-being.

5. Rituals and Ceremonies: Rituals and ceremonies are practices that are designed to mark significant life events or to honor something greater than oneself. They can take many forms, such as weddings, funerals, or religious ceremonies.

6. Sacred Texts and Literature: Sacred texts and literature are writings that are of great spiritual significance. They can provide guidance and inspiration for those seeking greater spiritual understanding and connection.

7. Creative Expression: Creative expression is a practice of using art, music, dance, or writing to express one's thoughts and emotions, and to connect with something greater than oneself.

8. Service and Giving Back: Service and giving back are practices that involve helping others and contributing to the greater good. These practices can help to develop greater empathy and compassion and promote a sense of connection to others and the world.

Spiritual practices can be powerful tools for awakening consciousness and promoting personal growth and well-being. By engaging in these practices, we can develop greater awareness of ourselves and the world around us, cultivate greater empathy and compassion, and connect to something greater than ourselves. In this chapter, we have explored what spiritual practices are, why they are important for awakening consciousness, and the different types of practices that will be covered in the following subsections. By exploring these practices and incorporating them into our daily lives, we can take a step towards greater spiritual understanding and connection.

Meditation

Meditation is a spiritual practice that has been around for thousands of years, with its roots in ancient Eastern traditions. The practice involves training the mind to focus and be present, which can lead to greater clarity, calmness, and a deeper connection to oneself and the world. In this subsection, we will delve into the history of meditation, explore different techniques, and discuss the benefits of meditation for awakening consciousness. We will also provide guidance on how to start a meditation practice and offer tips for maintaining a regular practice.

They have practiced meditation for thousands of years in various spiritual traditions. It has roots in ancient Hindu and Buddhist practices, but we also found it in Christianity, Judaism, and Islam. The practice of meditation involves sitting in a comfortable position, focusing on the breath, and observing the thoughts and emotions that arise without judgment. There are many techniques for meditation, each with its own unique approach and benefits.

One of the most popular techniques is mindfulness meditation. This technique involves focusing on the present moment, observing thoughts and sensations without judgment, and returning the focus to the breath when the mind wanders. They have shown mindfulness meditation to reduce stress and anxiety, improve mood and well-being, and increase attention and focus.

Another technique is mantra meditation. This technique involves repeating a word or phrase, such as "Om" or "peace," to help focus the mind and cultivate a sense of calmness and peace. They have shown mantra meditation to reduce stress, anxiety, and depression and promote feelings of well-being and relaxation.

The benefits of meditation for consciousness are vast. Regular meditation practice can lead to greater self-awareness and insight, improved emotional regulation, and increased compassion and empathy. It can also improve mental clarity, focus, and creativity, and promote overall well-being.

Getting started with meditation can be challenging, especially for beginners. The first step is to find a quiet, comfortable place to meditate. It is also important to set a regular time for meditation, whether it's in the morning or evening, and to commit to a daily practice. Starting with shorter meditation sessions, such as 5-10 minutes, and accumulating the time can also be helpful.

There are also many resources available to help beginners start a meditation practice, such as guided meditations, meditation apps, and classes. It's helpful to experiment with different techniques to find the one that works best for you. Maintaining a regular meditation practice can be challenging, but there are several tips that can help. Finding a community or accountability partner can provide motivation and support. Setting realistic goals and tracking progress can also help to stay on track. Consistency is key, so finding a routine that works for you and sticking to it can be the key to a successful meditation practice.

In conclusion, meditation is a powerful spiritual practice can promote personal growth, well-being, and awakening consciousness. By exploring the different techniques, benefits, and tips for starting and maintaining a regular practice, we can experience the transformative power of meditation in our lives.

Yoga

Yoga is a spiritual practice that has been around for thousands of years, with its roots in ancient Indian traditions. The practice involves physical postures, breathing techniques, and meditation to promote physical and spiritual well-being. There are many different styles of yoga, each with their own unique focus and benefits.

One of the most popular styles of yoga is Hatha yoga, which focuses on physical postures, or asanas, and breathing techniques, or pranayama. This style of yoga is great for beginners because it is slow-paced and gentle, but it can also be challenging for advanced practitioners who want to deepen their practice. Hatha yoga can improve flexibility, strength, balance, and posture, and it can also promote relaxation and stress relief.

Another style of yoga is Vinyasa yoga, which is more dynamic and fast-paced than Hatha yoga. Vinyasa yoga involves moving through a sequence of poses, or asanas, synchronized with the breath. This style of yoga can improve cardiovascular health, endurance, and strength, and it can also promote mental clarity and focus.

Kundalini yoga is a style of yoga that focuses on energy flow and chakra balancing. It involves physical postures, breathing techniques, and meditation, as well as chanting and mantra repetition. Kundalini yoga can promote spiritual awakening, self-awareness, and connection to the divine.

Restorative yoga is a style of yoga that involves relaxing poses held for extended periods of time, often supported by props such as blankets and bolsters. This style of yoga can promote deep relaxation, stress relief, and improved sleep.

The benefits of yoga for physical and spiritual well-being are vast. Regular yoga practice can improve flexibility, strength, balance, and posture, as well as promote relaxation, stress relief, and improved sleep. Yoga can also promote spiritual growth, self-awareness, and connection to the divine.

Getting started with yoga can be intimidating, especially for beginners. It is important to find a qualified teacher who can guide you through the practice and ensure proper alignment and safety. It is also important to listen to your body and practice at your own pace, taking breaks when needed and avoiding pushing yourself too hard.

There are also many resources available to help beginners start a yoga practice, such as yoga classes, online videos, and books. It can be helpful to experiment with different styles and teachers to find the one that works best for you. Maintaining a regular yoga practice can be challenging, but there are several tips that can help. Finding a community or accountability partner can provide motivation and support. Setting realistic goals and tracking progress can also help to stay on track. Consistency is key, so finding a routine that works for you and sticking to it can be the key to a successful yoga practice.

To sum up, yoga is a spiritual practice that can have a positive impact on both our physical and spiritual well-being. Through various yoga styles and techniques, we can experience the transformative power of yoga in our lives. Yoga is not just a physical exercise but a practice that can help us connect with our higher selves and the divine. It can also help us develop resilience and equanimity, as well as flexibility and strength in our minds and spirits. Additionally, yoga is a practice that can be adapted to meet the needs and abilities of any individual, and it can provide a sense of belonging and connection to a community of like-minded individuals. Whether we seek spiritual growth, physical health, or stress relief, committing to a regular yoga practice can help us unlock the full potential of this ancient practice and experience greater fulfillment and joy in our lives.

Mindfulness

Mindfulness is a powerful practice that can help us become more present and aware in our lives. By cultivating greater awareness of our thoughts, emotions, and bodily sensations in the present moment, we can learn to live more fully and authentically, and experience greater joy, peace, and fulfillment. The practice of mindfulness can take many forms, but it is often associated with meditation. Mindfulness meditation involves sitting in a comfortable position and focusing on the breath, or on a particular object or sensation. As thoughts and distractions arise, we simply observe them without judgment and return our attention to the present moment.

Mindfulness can also apply to our daily activities, such as eating, walking, or working. By bringing our full attention and awareness to these activities, we can experience them more fully and with greater appreciation. For example, when eating, we can savor the flavors and textures of the food and be fully present with each bite. When walking, we can feel the sensations of the ground beneath our feet and notice the sights and sounds around us.

The benefits of mindfulness are numerous and well-documented. By developing greater awareness and presence, we can reduce stress and anxiety, improve our relationships, and enhance our overall well-being. Mindfulness can also help us to cultivate greater self-awareness and self-acceptance, and to develop greater compassion and empathy for others.

One of the most beautiful aspects of mindfulness is that it is a practice that can be integrated into any aspect of our lives. Whether we are at work, at home, or in a social setting, we can bring our full attention and presence to the moment, and experience greater joy and fulfillment as a result. However, like any practice, mindfulness requires commitment and effort. It can be challenging to cultivate greater awareness and presence in a world that is so full of distractions and stimuli. But with dedication and practice, we can learn to cultivate greater mindfulness and presence in our lives and experience the many benefits that come with this powerful practice.

To sum up, mindfulness is a practice that involves developing greater awareness and presence in our lives, both through meditation and our daily activities. This heightened awareness allows us to become more attuned to our thoughts, emotions, and bodily sensations in the present moment, which can lead to greater fulfillment, compassion, and empathy.

If you're new to mindfulness, there are various resources available to help you start, such as attending workshops, seeking out qualified mentors, or using apps and online resources. However, it's essential to begin small and remain consistent with your practice. Gradually increasing the time you spend in mindfulness each day can lead to a profound impact on your well-being and consciousness. It's important to remember that mindfulness is a lifelong practice that requires continuous effort and commitment. As you continue to practice mindfulness, you may notice a deepening of your awareness and presence, leading to a greater sense of inner peace, contentment, and fulfillment.

In conclusion, mindfulness is a potent practice that enables us to cultivate a deeper sense of awareness and presence in our lives, ultimately resulting in greater joy, peace, and fulfillment. By dedicating yourself to this practice and utilizing available resources, you can reap the many benefits that mindfulness has to offer.

Breathwork

Breathwork is a powerful practice that has been used for centuries to promote physical, emotional, and spiritual well-being. It involves the use of specific breathing techniques to regulate the breath and promote relaxation, calmness, and inner peace. There are many breathwork practices, each with their own unique focus and benefits.

I know one of the most common types of breathwork as "diaphragmatic breathing" or "belly breathing." This involves inhaling deeply through the nose, filling the lungs and belly with air, and then exhaling slowly through the mouth, allowing the belly to deflate.

They have shown this type of breathing to reduce stress, lower blood pressure, and promote relaxation and well-being.

We know another type of breathwork as "pranayama," which is a term used in yoga to describe various breathing techniques. Some pranayama techniques involve breathing in specific patterns, such as inhaling for a certain number of counts and then exhaling for a longer count. Other techniques involve holding the breath for a period or breathing through alternate nostrils.

Breathwork can also involve more intense techniques, such as "breath of fire," which involves rapid, forceful breathing through the nose. This type of breathwork can invigorate and energizing and is often used in yoga and other spiritual practices to help awaken the body and mind.

Whatever type of breathwork you choose to practice, it is important to start slowly and be mindful of your body's responses. Start with just a few minutes of deep breathing each day, escalating the time you spend in practice as you become more comfortable.

One of the great things about breathwork is that we can practice anywhere it. Whether you are sitting at your desk, standing in line at the grocery store, or lying in bed before sleep, you can use breathwork to promote relaxation, reduce stress, and cultivate greater well-being. Breathwork is a powerful practice that can help us regulate our breath and promote greater physical, emotional, and spiritual well-being. Whether through diaphragmatic breathing, pranayama, or more intense techniques, breathwork can be an effective tool for reducing stress, anxiety, and depression, and promoting greater relaxation and inner peace. If you are interested in exploring the many benefits of breathwork, there are many resources available to help you get started, and with dedication and practice, you can experience the many benefits that come with this powerful practice.

Rituals and Ceremonies

Rituals and ceremonies are an integral part of many cultures and traditions around the world. They mark important life events, such as births, weddings, and funerals, as well as to honor something greater than oneself, such as a deity or a spiritual belief.

One of the main purposes of rituals and ceremonies is to create a sense of meaning and purpose in life. They allow individuals to connect with something larger than themselves and to feel a sense of belonging to a community or group. Rituals and ceremonies can also provide a sense of comfort and solace during times of hardship or loss.

Weddings are a common example of a ritual or ceremony. They often involve specific traditions and customs, such as exchanging vows and rings, sharing a meal with family and friends, and performing a first dance. These traditions not only provide structure and meaning to the wedding ceremony, but they also serve to connect the couple to their cultural and religious heritage.

Funerals are another example of a ritual or ceremony. They provide an opportunity for family and friends to come together to honor the life of the deceased and to support each other during the grieving process. Rituals and traditions, such as laying flowers on the casket or sharing memories of the deceased, can help to create a sense of closure and provide comfort to those who are grieving.

Religious ceremonies are also an important aspect of many spiritual practices. They may involve specific prayers, rituals, and customs that are designed to connect individuals with their faith and to honor their spiritual beliefs. For example, in the Christian tradition, attending church services and participating in sacraments such as baptism and communion are important rituals that serve to deepen an individual's connection to God.

In addition to marking significant life events, rituals and ceremonies can also be used as a tool for personal growth and transformation. Many spiritual traditions use rituals and ceremonies to connect with the divine and to access higher states of consciousness. These practices can include meditation, chanting, and other forms of spiritual discipline.

Overall, rituals and ceremonies are an important part of spiritual practices and can serve as a powerful tool for personal growth and transformation. They provide structure, meaning, and purpose to life, and can help individuals to connect with something greater than themselves. Whether through weddings, funerals, or religious ceremonies, rituals and ceremonies are an important aspect of many cultures and traditions around the world.

Sacred Texts and Literature

Sacred texts and literature have played a significant role in the development of many spiritual traditions. These texts are often considered to be the word of the divine and are revered for their ability to provide guidance and wisdom to those seeking a deeper connection to the spiritual realm.

There are many sacred texts and literature, each with their own unique characteristics and messages. Some of the most well-known include the Bible, the Quran, the Bhagavad Gita, and the Tao Te Ching. These texts are the foundational works of many of the world's major religions and are still widely read and studied today.

One of the key benefits of studying sacred texts and literature is the insights they can provide into the divine. These texts often contain stories, parables, and teachings that provide guidance on how to live a life that is aligned with the will of the divine. They can also offer a greater understanding of the universe and the human experience and can provide comfort and solace during times of hardship.

Besides providing guidance and wisdom, sacred texts and literature can also help to foster a sense of community and shared identity among followers of a particular spiritual tradition. Reading and studying these texts can be a way for individuals to connect with others who share their beliefs and values and can provide a sense of belonging and connection to something greater than oneself.

While the study of sacred texts and literature is often associated with religious traditions, it can also be a valuable practice for those who identify as spiritual but not religious. Many spiritual texts offer insights into consciousness, the interconnectedness of all things, and the importance of living a life of compassion and service. By studying these texts, individuals can deepen their understanding of their own spiritual path and find inspiration for their own journey towards greater consciousness.

It is important to note that we should approach the study of sacred texts and literature with an open mind and a spirit of inquiry. While these texts are of great spiritual significance, they were also written within a specific cultural and historical context. It is important to consider the cultural and historical context in which they were written, and to approach them with a critical eye to fully understand their message and significance.

In conclusion, the study of sacred texts and literature can be a valuable practice for those seeking greater spiritual understanding and connection. These texts offer guidance, wisdom, and inspiration, and can help to foster a sense of community and shared identity among followers of a particular spiritual tradition. By approaching these texts with an open mind and a spirit of inquiry, individuals can deepen their understanding of their own spiritual path and find inspiration for their own journey towards greater consciousness.

Creative Expression

Creative expression is a powerful tool for self-discovery and spiritual growth. It allows individuals to explore their inner selves, express their emotions, and connect with their spirituality. There are many forms of creative expression, including art, music, dance, writing, and more. Each form offers its unique benefits and can support spiritual practices.

Art, for example, can be meditation in which individuals can focus their minds and emotions on the creative process. The act of creating can be cathartic, allowing individuals to release emotions and gain a deeper understanding of their inner selves. We can also use art as a tool for self-reflection and exploration, as individuals can use their creations to gain insight into their inner world.

Music and dance can also be powerful tools for spiritual growth. These forms of expression allow individuals to connect with their bodies and emotions, tapping into their innermost thoughts and feelings. Through music and dance, individuals can achieve a greater sense of mindfulness and presence, connecting with the present moment and the greater universe.

Writing is another form of creative expression that can support spiritual practices. Writing can be used for self-reflection, allowing individuals to explore their thoughts and emotions and gain a deeper understanding of themselves. It can also be used for manifestation, as individuals can write down their goals and desires to help bring them to fruition.

Creative expression can also be used as a means of connecting with others and building community. Through shared creative experiences, individuals can support one another in their spiritual journeys, fostering a sense of connection and belonging.

Incorporating creative expression into one's spiritual practices can be a powerful way to deepen one's connection to the universe and to oneself. It allows individuals to tap into their inner creativity, express their emotions, and connect with something greater than themselves. Whether through art, music, dance, writing, or other forms of expression, creative practices can support spiritual growth and lead to a more fulfilling and meaningful life.

Service and Giving Back

Service and giving back are practices that involve helping others and contributing to the greater good. These practices can take many forms, from volunteering at a local charity to participating in a community service project. When we engage in service and giving back, we can connect with something greater than ourselves and make a positive impact on the world.

One of the benefits of service and giving back is that it can help to develop greater empathy and compassion. By helping others, we can put ourselves in their shoes and understand their struggles and challenges. This can help to break down barriers and promote greater understanding and connection between people of different backgrounds and experiences.

Service and giving back can also promote a sense of connection to others and the world. When we engage in these practices, we can see the impact of our actions and the difference that we are making in the lives of others. This can help to give us a greater sense of purpose and meaning in our lives and can motivate us to continue making a positive impact.

There are many ways to engage in service and giving back, and it is important to find a way that resonates with us personally. Some people may choose to volunteer at a local charity, while others may participate in a community service project or donate to a cause that they are passionate about. Whatever form it takes, the important thing is to find a way to give back that feels meaningful and fulfilling.

It is also important to remember that service and giving back are not just about helping others – they can also be incredibly rewarding for us personally. When we engage in these practices, we can tap into a sense of generosity and kindness that can bring us great joy and fulfillment. By giving back to others, we can cultivate a sense of abundance and gratitude in our lives, and to see the world in a more positive and hopeful light.

In conclusion, service and giving back are powerful practices that can help us to connect with something greater than ourselves, develop greater empathy and compassion, and make a positive impact on the world. Whether we choose to volunteer, donate, or participate in a community service project, these practices can bring us great joy and fulfillment, and help us to see the world in a more positive and hopeful light

8

Power of Intention

Intention is a powerful tool that can help us create the life we want and manifest our desires. Our thoughts and actions are guided by our intentions, and when we set clear and focused intentions, we are better able to achieve our goals and live a fulfilling life.

The first step in harnessing the power of intention is to become clear about what we truly want. This involves taking the time to reflect on our deepest desires and values, and then setting specific, measurable, and achievable goals that align with these aspirations. It's important to remember that our intentions must come from a place of authenticity and alignment with our true selves, rather than being driven by external pressures or societal expectations. Once we have set our intentions, we must also cultivate the belief that we can achieve them. This involves letting go of limiting beliefs and negative self-talk, and instead focusing on our strengths and potential. Visualization and affirmation practices can be helpful in strengthening our belief in ourselves and our ability to manifest our intentions.

Acting towards our intentions is also crucial for their manifestation. This involves pursuing our goals and taking steps towards them, rather than waiting for things to happen to us. It's important to remain flexible and adaptable, and to be open to new opportunities and experiences that may help us achieve our intentions in unexpected ways. Another key aspect of the power of intention is the role of energy and vibration. Everything in the universe comprises energy, and our thoughts and emotions emit their own vibrations that can attract or repel certain experiences and outcomes. By focusing our thoughts and emotions on positive and high-frequency vibrations, such as love, gratitude, and joy, we can attract similar experiences and opportunities into our lives.

To fully harness the power of intention, it's important to cultivate a daily practice of mindfulness, gratitude, and self-reflection. This can involve meditation, journaling, or other practices that help us stay present and connected to our intentions and our inner selves. It's also important to surround ourselves with a supportive and positive like-minded people that encourages us to stay committed to our intentions and holds us accountable.

The Importance of Setting Clear and Authentic Intentions

For the power of intention, setting clear and authentic intentions is key. To manifest what we truly desire, we must first have a clear idea of what that is. This requires us to be honest with ourselves about what we want and why we want it. Setting apparent intentions can help us focus our energy and attention on what truly matters, and to let go of distractions and doubts that can hold us back. It can also help us stay motivated and committed to our goals, even when faced with obstacles or setbacks.

However, it is important to remember that our intentions should be authentic and aligned with our true values and purpose. If we set intentions that are based on external pressures or expectations, we may find ourselves feeling unfulfilled or disconnected from our true selves.

To set clear and authentic intentions, it's helpful to take some time to reflect on our values, desires, and goals. We can ask ourselves questions like: What do I truly want to achieve? Why is this important to me? How does it align with my values and purpose?

Once we have a clear idea of our intentions, we can write them down or create visual reminders to help us stay focused and motivated. It can also be helpful to share our intentions with others who support us, as this can help to create accountability and positive energy around our goals. Ultimately, setting clear and authentic intentions can help us to manifest our deepest desires and live a more purposeful and fulfilling life.

Cultivating Belief in Ourselves and Our Ability to Manifest our Intentions.

When it comes to setting intentions, cultivating a belief in ourselves and our ability to manifest them is crucial. Without this belief, our intentions can become mere wishes or dreams that never come to fruition. Believing in ourselves means trusting that we have the power to create the reality we desire. It means recognizing our strengths and abilities and having faith in our capacity to overcome obstacles and challenges.

To cultivate this belief, we must first let go of any limiting beliefs or self-doubt that may hold us back. We can do this by examining our thoughts and questioning whether they are serving us or hindering us. We can also practice positive self-talk and affirmations, reminding ourselves of our worth and capabilities. Visualizing ourselves successfully manifesting our intentions can also help to reinforce this belief.

Another way to cultivate belief is through acting towards our intentions. When we take steps towards our goals, even small ones, it can increase our confidence and sense of empowerment. Celebrating our successes along the way can also help to reinforce our belief in ourselves. Encouraging belief in ourselves and our ability to manifest our intentions is a practice that requires consistent effort and self-reflection. It's challenging to create but the rewards are invaluable to design the life we truly desire. The next sections will help you understand.

Acting towards our intentions

Acting towards our intentions is a crucial step in manifesting our desires and achieving our goals. It is not enough to simply set our intentions and hope for the best—we must also take deliberate and consistent action towards realizing our vision. Taking action can be challenging, as it often requires us to step outside of our comfort zones and confront our fears and limiting beliefs. However, when we approach action with a sense of courage and determination, we can make incredible progress towards our goals.

One key to taking effective action is to break down our goals into smaller, more manageable steps. By setting achievable milestones, we can build momentum and stay motivated as we work towards our ultimate vision. It can also be helpful to enlist the support of others, whether through accountability partnerships, mentorship, or simply sharing our goals with trusted friends and family members.

Another important aspect of acting towards our intentions is to remain flexible and adaptable. Often, our paths towards our goals will require us to pivot, adjust our course, or even completely change direction. By remaining open to new possibilities and learning from our experiences, we can stay on track towards our ultimate vision, even in the face of unexpected challenges or setbacks.

It is crucial to approach our actions with a grateful attitude, appreciating the resources and opportunities available to us. By adopting a positive outlook and focusing on the favorable aspects of our journey, we can remain inspired and motivated, even when faced with challenging situations.

To summarize, taking action towards our intentions is a vital part of realizing our aspirations and accomplishing our objectives. We can achieve this by breaking down our goals into manageable steps, seeking the assistance of others, remaining adaptable and flexible, and fostering an attitude of thankfulness. With these approaches, we can make substantial progress towards our ultimate vision.

Energy and Vibration

In manifesting our intentions, it's not just about setting clear goals and acting towards them. Another important factor to consider is the role of energy and vibration.

Everything in the universe comprises energy, including our thoughts and emotions. When we focus our thoughts and emotions towards a specific intention, we are creating a certain vibration or frequency that attracts similar energy and circumstances into our lives.

For example, if we focus on feelings of gratitude and abundance, we are creating a positive vibration that can attract more abundance and prosperity into our lives. If we focus on feelings of lack and scarcity, we are creating a negative vibration that can attract more of the same into our lives.

Therefore, it's important to not only set clear and authentic intentions but also to cultivate positive energy and vibration around them. We can do this through practices such as meditation, visualization, affirmations, and gratitude. Meditation can help us quiet our minds and cultivate a sense of inner peace and calm. This can help to increase our overall energy and vibration, making it easier to align with our intentions. Visualization involves creating a mental image of ourselves already achieving our intention. This can help to create a positive energy and vibration around our goal, making it more likely to manifest. Affirmations involve repeating positive statements to ourselves that align with our intentions. This can help to shift our mindset towards a more positive and empowered state, increasing our energy and vibration around our goal.

Gratitude involves focusing on the things we already have in our lives and expressing gratitude for them. This can help to cultivate a sense of abundance and positivity, increasing our overall energy and vibration.

By understanding the role of energy and vibration in intention manifestation, we can become more intentional about the thoughts and emotions we cultivate in our goals. This can help us create a more positive and empowered mindset and ultimately manifest our intentions more easily and effectively.

Community

With setting and achieving intentions, having a supportive community can make all the difference. The people we surround ourselves with can either lift us up or bring us down, so it's important to choose our circle wisely.

One way that community can support us in our intentions is by providing encouragement and accountability. When we share our goals and aspirations with others, they can offer words of encouragement and support, and hold us accountable for following through on our commitments. This can be especially helpful when we may feel discouraged or overwhelmed. Being part of a community can provide us with opportunities for growth and learning. We can learn from the experiences and insights of others and receive valuable feedback and guidance. Being part of a community can also help us expand our perspectives and challenge our assumptions, which can be critical for personal and spiritual growth.

There are many ways to cultivate community support for our intentions. Joining a spiritual or personal development group, attending workshops or retreats, and seeking like-minded individuals can all be effective ways to build a supportive community. It's important to be intentional about creating these connections and relationships, and to approach them with an open and curious mindset. The role of community in supporting our intentions is about creating a space where we can be ourselves, share our experiences and insights, and receive support and guidance as we navigate the journey of awakening consciousness. With the help of a supportive community, we can stay connected to our inner selves, stay focused on our intentions, and continue to grow and develop along the way.

9

The Nature of Reality

Have you ever stopped to ponder the nature of reality? What is it, really? Is it what we see, feel, and touch, or is there something more profound and intangible than that? In this chapter, we'll delve into reality and explore how our perceptions and beliefs shape our experiences.

What is Reality?

At its core, reality refers to the state of things as they exist, independent of our perceptions and beliefs. However, the way we perceive and interpret reality can vary widely based on our individual experiences, beliefs, and perspectives. For example, red may look different to you than it does to someone else, based on differences in our eyes' ability to see color or cultural associations with the color red. In this way, a multitude of factors shape our perception of reality beyond what we can physically see or touch.

Perception and Belief

Our perceptions and beliefs play a crucial role in shaping our experiences of reality. Our beliefs act as filters that determine what we perceive as real or unreal, important, or unimportant, and meaningful or meaningless. For example, if we believe that the world is a dangerous and unforgiving place, we may perceive threats and danger around every corner. In contrast, if we believe that the world is a kind place, we may perceive acts of kindness and love more readily.

Therefore, it's essential to cultivate self-awareness and examine our beliefs to ensure that they align with our desires and intentions. By doing so, we can consciously shape our experiences and create a more fulfilling and joyful reality.

The Illusion of Separation

One of the fundamental principles of reality is that everything is interdependent. However, we often operate under the illusion of separation, believing that we are separate from others and the world. This illusion of separation leads to feelings of isolation, fear, and disconnection. It's only when we recognize the interconnectedness of all things that we can truly understand our place in the world and our connection to something greater than ourselves.

The Power of Perception Shifts

One of the most significant insights we can gain from exploring reality is that our perceptions are malleable. By shifting our perceptions, we can transform our experiences of reality and create a more positive and fulfilling life. For example, if we shift our perception of a challenge as an opportunity for growth, we can approach it with a sense of curiosity and openness rather than fear and resistance.

The nature of reality is complex and multifaceted, shaped by our perceptions and beliefs, and influenced by a myriad of external factors. However, by cultivating self-awareness, recognizing the illusion of separation, and shifting our perceptions, we can create a more joyful and fulfilling reality.

Defining Nature in Reality

To fully understand the nature of reality, it is important to consider different perspectives and philosophies. Many ancient spiritual traditions view reality as an interconnected web of energy and consciousness, while modern physics suggests that reality is made up of vibrating energy fields. From a spiritual perspective, we often see reality as a reflection of our inner state of being. Our thoughts, emotions, and beliefs can shape our external reality. We express this idea in the law of attraction, which states that like attracts like. If we focus on positive thoughts and emotions, we can attract positive experiences into our lives.

Some scientific theories suggest our perceptions and observations shape that reality. The famous double-slit experiment in quantum mechanics shows the observer has a direct impact on the behavior of subatomic particles. This suggests that our perception and observation of reality can influence its manifestation. Regardless of one's philosophical or scientific perspective, the nature of reality is complex and multifaceted. Understanding the nature of reality can help us to develop a greater sense of awareness and consciousness, and to navigate the world in a more mindful and intentional way.

Furthermore, the nature of reality can be explored through various philosophical and spiritual frameworks. Some believe in the concept of dualism, where reality is composed of two opposing forces such as good and evil, mind and matter, or body and soul. Others subscribe to monism, where reality is seen as a unified whole, with all things connected and inseparable.

Another way of looking at the nature of reality is through the lens of quantum physics, which challenges our traditional understanding of reality as a solid, predictable, and objective phenomenon. Quantum physics suggests that reality is more fluid, and that observation and perception can influence and shape the outcome of events.

Ultimately, the nature of reality is a complex and multifaceted concept that can be understood through different perspectives and disciplines. Whether we view reality as subjective or objective, dualistic or unified, or physical or spiritual, our perception and understanding of reality can greatly influence our thoughts, beliefs, and actions.

Perception and Reality: How We Experience the World

Our perception of the world is shaped by our experiences, beliefs, and cultural conditioning. It's easy to assume that our perception is reality, but in truth, what we see is just one interpretation of a vast and complex reality. Our perception is influenced by our individual perspective, which is limited by our senses and subjective experiences. For example, two people can witness the same event and come away with different perceptions of what happened. This is because our brains interpret sensory information based on our past experiences and beliefs. Our perception of reality is a construct of our minds, rather than an objective truth.

This realization can be both liberating and challenging. On one hand, it means that we have the power to shape our perception of reality by changing our beliefs and thought patterns. On the other hand, it can be difficult to recognize the limitations of our perception and be open to alternative viewpoints. To truly awaken our consciousness, we must be willing to examine our perceptions and question their validity. By doing so, we can expand our understanding of reality and become more compassionate and empathetic towards others who may have different perceptions of the world.

Our perception shapes our reality. How we see the world is unique to everyone, and it affects how we interact with others and the world around us. Perception can be influenced by our beliefs, values, experiences, and emotions. Our brain is constantly processing information and making sense of the world. It filters out some information and highlights others based on our interests, needs, and expectations. This filtering process can create biases in our perception, which may not accurately reflect reality. Our emotions can also influence our perception of the world. When we are feeling happy, we may see the world in a more positive light, whereas when we are feeling sad or anxious, our perception may be more negative.

It is important to be aware of our perception and how it shapes our reality. By recognizing our biases and emotional influences, we can work to expand our perspective and gain a more accurate understanding of the world. This can help us communicate more effectively with others, make better decisions, and cultivate a greater sense of empathy and understanding.

Our perception of reality can be influenced by our experiences, cultural background, and personal biases. These factors can shape our beliefs and perspectives, leading to different interpretations of the same event or situation. It's important to recognize that our perception of reality is subjective and may not always align with objective truth. However, by noticing our biases and examining our beliefs, we can gain a deeper understanding of ourselves and the world.

Our senses, emotions, and cognitive processes shape our perception of reality. Our experiences and personal biases can also influence it. By realizing these factors and examining our beliefs, we can gain a deeper understanding of ourselves and the world.

The Role of Consciousness

Our consciousness plays a crucial role in shaping our reality. It is through our consciousness that we perceive the world, interpret information, and decide. Our thoughts and beliefs also influence how we perceive reality and can shape our experiences. For example, if we hold a belief that we cannot achieve something, we may be less likely to act towards that goal and may even subconsciously sabotage our efforts. If we hold a belief that we are capable and deserving of success, we may be more likely to act and create opportunities for ourselves.

Our consciousness also could affect the energy and vibration around us, which can influence the events and circumstances that manifest in our lives. This is the principle behind the law of attraction, which states that we attract what we focus on and believe in. Therefore, by cultivating a positive and empowered mindset, we can shift our consciousness towards a state of abundance and possibility and create a reality that aligns with our intentions and desires. Conversely, if we allow ourselves to dwell in negative thoughts and beliefs, we may unknowingly attract experiences that reflect those same patterns.

It is important to note, however, that our consciousness alone cannot control every aspect of reality. There are external factors and forces that are beyond our control, such as natural disasters or the actions of others. But by cultivating a conscious and intentional approach to our thoughts and beliefs, we can better navigate and respond to the circumstances that arise in our lives.

Quantum Physics and Nature of Reality

Quantum physics is a branch of physics that studies the behavior of matter and energy on a tiny scale. In recent years, it has gained a lot of attention for its implications for reality. According to quantum physics, reality is not fixed and deterministic, but is probabilistic and dependent on observation.

Quantum mechanics suggests particles do not have definite properties until they are observed or measured. We know this as the observer effect. Particles can exist in multiple states at once until we observe them, and then they collapse into a single state. This means that the act of observation has a fundamental role in shaping reality.

Quantum physics suggests that everything in the universe is interconnected and entangled. This means that particles can instantaneously influence each other, regardless of the distance between them.

This interconnectedness implies that we are not separate from our reality, but it intimately connected us to it.

The implications of quantum physics for reality are profound. It suggests that reality is not objective and fixed but is shaped by our observations and consciousness. This means that we have the power to shape our reality through our thoughts, beliefs, and intentions. It also implies that everything in the universe connects, and that we are part of a larger whole. Quantum physics has challenged our traditional understanding of reality, introducing the idea that particles can exist in multiple states at once and that observation can affect the behavior of particles. This has led some scientists and philosophers to speculate that consciousness may play a fundamental role in shaping reality.

One popular interpretation of quantum physics, known as the Copenhagen interpretation, suggests that reality is not determined until we observed it. Particles exist in a state of superposition until they are observed or measured, at which point they "collapse" into a definite state. This has led some to suggest that consciousness may be involved in the process of observation and measurement and may even be fundamental to reality itself. While the idea that consciousness plays a fundamental role in shaping reality is still highly debated, our understanding of reality is constantly developing. As we continue to explore the nature of consciousness and the workings of the universe, we may discover new insights that challenge our current beliefs and open new avenues of exploration and discovery.

Beyond the Physical: Exploring the Spiritual Dimensions of Reality

When we think of reality, we often focus on the physical world around us. But there is a spiritual dimension to reality that is just as important to explore. This spiritual dimension can encompass everything from our connection to a higher power to our sense of purpose and meaning in life.

Many people turn to spirituality to explore this deeper level of reality. This can involve practices like meditation, prayer, or ritual, which can help us connect with a sense of the divine or the transcendent. It can also involve exploring our own inner landscape, examining our beliefs, values, and desires to better understand our place in the world. One key aspect of the spiritual dimension of reality is the idea of interconnectedness. This suggests that everything in the universe is connected, and that we are all part of a larger, unified whole. This can be a powerful realization, as it can help us see our own lives and experiences in a broader context. It can also help us feel more connected to the world around us, and to other people.

Another important aspect of the spiritual dimension of reality is the idea of purpose. Many people find that exploring their spiritual beliefs can help them better understand their own sense of purpose and meaning in life. This can involve asking questions like: What am I here to do? What is my role in the world? How can I make a positive impact?

Ultimately, exploring the spiritual dimensions of reality can be a deeply rewarding and transformative experience. By opening ourselves up to the possibility of something greater than us, we can gain a new perspective on our lives and our place in the world. We can also deepen our sense of connection to others, and to the world around us. Many spiritual traditions and practices recognize that there are dimensions of reality beyond the physical realm. These dimensions are often referred to as spiritual, energetic, or metaphysical. They may include concepts such as the soul, spirit, consciousness, and energy.

In these traditions, it is believed that the physical world is just one aspect of reality and that there are other dimensions that are equally important. These dimensions may be experienced through practices such as meditation, prayer, and energy work. By connecting with these dimensions, individuals may gain a deeper understanding of themselves and the world around them. Some spiritual traditions also recognize the interconnectedness of all things and the idea that everything is made up of the same energy or consciousness. This concept is often referred to as oneness or unity consciousness. It suggests that everything in the universe is interconnected and that there is no separation between individuals or between individuals and the environment.

In recent years, scientific research has also begun to explore the connection between spirituality and the nature of reality. Studies have shown that practices such as meditation and energy work can have measurable effects on the brain and body, suggesting that there may be a tangible connection between the physical and spiritual dimensions of reality.

Overall, exploring the spiritual dimensions of reality can be a powerful way to cultivate a deeper understanding of the world and us. It can help us to connect with something greater than ourselves and to recognize our interconnectedness with all things.

Reality and Perception of Time: Is Time Real?

Our perception of time is an interesting aspect of our reality. We often talk about time as if it is a tangible thing that can be measured, but time is a concept that we use to organize our experience of the world. Some scientists and philosophers argue that time is an illusion, and that it does not actually exist in the way that we think it does. They suggest that our experience of time is created by our perception of change in the world around us. In other words, we experience time because things happen, and we can remember them happening.

Others argue that time is real, but that it is a relative concept. The way we experience time can be influenced by a variety of factors, including our state of consciousness, our location in the universe, and even our emotions.

For example, if you are waiting for something exciting to happen, time may seem to pass more slowly than if you are engaged in an activity that you enjoy. Similarly, time can seem to pass more quickly when we are in a state of flow, fully engaged in an activity that we find challenging and rewarding.

Ultimately, the nature of time and its relationship to reality is still the subject of much debate and exploration. As we continue to learn more about the nature of the universe and our place in it, we may gain new insights into the true nature of time and its role in shaping our experience of reality. As a result of these studies, some scientists have suggested that time may be an illusion created by the limitations of our human perception. This idea is further supported by certain spiritual and philosophical traditions, which propose that time is a construct of the mind, and that true reality exists beyond the constraints of time.

Regardless of whether time is ultimately deemed to be real or illusory, the fact remains that our perception of time has a profound impact on how we experience reality. By becoming more aware of our relationship with time and exploring different ways of perceiving it, we may be able to unlock new dimensions of reality and expand our consciousness in profound ways.

The Mystery of Existence: The Search for Meaning in Life

The search for meaning and purpose in life is a fundamental aspect of human existence. Throughout history, people have sought to understand the mysteries of existence and the purpose of their existence. Many philosophical and spiritual traditions offer their own interpretations of the meaning of life, but ultimately, the search for meaning is a deeply personal and subjective journey. For some, the search for meaning is tied to religious or spiritual beliefs. They may believe that their purpose in life is to serve a higher power or to follow a particular path of enlightenment. Others may find meaning in their relationships with others, their career, or their passions and hobbies.

Regardless of the source of meaning, the search for it can provide a sense of purpose and direction in life. It can help us prioritize our values and make choices that align with our beliefs and goals. It can also offer a sense of comfort and hope in the face of life's challenges and uncertainties. However, the search for meaning can also be a source of frustration and confusion. It is not always easy to know what we want or what our purpose is, and it's difficult to reconcile our personal beliefs and values with the demands of society and the world.

Ultimately, the search for meaning is a journey that requires patience, self-reflection, and an openness to new experiences and perspectives. It is a journey that may have no clear destination, but that can offer substantial rewards along the way. As we continue to explore the nature of reality, we inevitably come across the age-old question of the meaning of life. What is our purpose? What is the point of it all? While many religions and philosophical traditions offer their own answers, the search for meaning remains an elusive and deeply personal endeavor.

One perspective is that meaning is not inherent in the universe, but something we create ourselves. We can find purpose in our relationships, our work, our passions, or our contributions to the world. We can also find meaning in moments of transcendence, such as in nature, art, or spiritual experiences.

Another perspective is that meaning is a product of our own consciousness. It is not something we find, but something we bring to the world. In this view, we are not passive observers of reality, but active co-creators. Regardless of one's beliefs, the search for meaning can be a powerful driving force in our lives. It can inspire us to pursue our dreams, connect with others, and make a positive impact on the world. And as we continue to explore the nature of reality and the mysteries of existence, it is perhaps this search for meaning that gives us the most profound insights into our true nature and the nature of the world.

Living with an Awakened Consciousness: Embracing the Paradoxes of Reality

As we explore the nature of reality, we may find ourselves faced with paradoxes that challenge our understanding and push us to expand our consciousness. One of the most profound paradoxes is the idea that everything is interconnected and yet we are also individual beings with our own unique experiences. To live with an awakened consciousness is to embrace these paradoxes and hold them in balance. It is to recognize that while we are all part of a larger whole, we also have the power to shape our individual realities through our thoughts, beliefs, and actions.

Embracing the paradoxes of reality also means accepting that there may be aspects of the universe and our existence that we cannot fully understand or explain. This can be both humbling and awe-inspiring, as we realize the vastness and complexity of the universe. Living with an awakened consciousness also requires us to let go of the need for certainty and control. Instead, we must learn to trust in the unfolding of life and be open to the unexpected. We must see the world with fresh eyes and be open to new possibilities and perspectives.

Ultimately, living with an awakened consciousness means being fully present in the moment and embracing the mystery and wonder of existence. It is a journey of continual growth and evolution, as we learn to expand our consciousness and deepen our connection to our world.

As we deepen our understanding of reality, we may encounter paradoxes that challenge our assumptions and beliefs. These paradoxes may include concepts such as unity and diversity, free will and determinism, and form and emptiness.

One paradox we may encounter is the interplay between form and emptiness. On one hand, we experience the world through the forms and structures that we perceive, such as objects, people, and events. These forms are ultimately empty of inherent existence and are constantly changing. To embrace this paradox, we can cultivate an awareness of both the form and emptiness aspects of reality. We can appreciate the beauty and uniqueness of the forms we encounter, while also recognizing their impermanence and interdependence. This awareness can lead to a deeper sense of connection and compassion for all beings, as we recognize our shared nature and interconnectedness.

Another paradox we may encounter is the relationship between individuality and interconnectedness. On the one hand, we may experience a sense of separation and individuality as we navigate our own unique paths in life. We are also deeply interconnected with all beings and the world. To embrace this paradox, we can cultivate an awareness of both our individuality and our interconnectedness. We can honor and celebrate our unique identities and experiences, while also recognizing how we are all connected and interdependent. This awareness can lead to a greater sense of empathy and compassion for others, as we recognize our shared humanity and the struggles and joys that we all experience.

Living with an awakened consciousness involves embracing these paradoxes and holding them in a state of dynamic tension. It involves cultivating a deep sense of awareness and presence in each moment, as we navigate the complexities and mysteries of reality. Through this process, we can awaken to the fullness of our own being and our interconnectedness with all that is.

10

The Journey Continues

The pursuit of awakened consciousness is an ongoing journey that requires commitment and effort. As we progress further in our spiritual journey, we encounter fresh challenges, opportunities, and insights. This chapter delves into the nature of this never-ending journey and how to maintain purpose and clarity. It is vital to comprehend that the journey towards spiritual awakening is a continuous process that never really ends, even for those who have attained high levels of enlightenment. This is because life is constantly changing, and our spiritual journey involves learning from these changes and adapting to them. To continue growing on our journey, it is important to embrace the process itself, rather than just focusing on the destination.

While having goals and aspirations is essential, genuine transformation arises from fully immersing ourselves in each moment and learning from the experiences that present themselves.

Remaining open and curious about the world around us is key to ongoing growth on our awakening transformation. This means approaching each day with a sense of wonder and exploring new ideas, experiences, and perspectives. By remaining receptive to new possibilities, we can expand our consciousness and deepen our understanding of the world.

Practicing Mindfulness

The practice of mindfulness is a valuable tool for progressing on our journey. By being present in the moment and observing our thoughts and feelings without judgment, we can gain clarity and insight into our inner world. This can aid us in identifying areas where we can improve and grow, and in developing greater self-awareness. It is crucial to bear in mind that our journey towards awakened consciousness is a continuous process of learning and development. Even as we attain higher levels of enlightenment and consciousness, there is always more to discover and comprehend. By remaining dedicated to our path and seeking out new opportunities for growth and learning, we can keep evolving and surmounting our limitations. The journey towards awakened consciousness is a process of growth and transformation that is life changing. By embracing the journey, itself, staying receptive and curious, practicing mindfulness, and continuing to learn and develop, we can deepen our understanding of ourselves and our reality. May this book inspire you to persist in your journey with purpose, passion, and clarity, and to accept the perpetual path of transcendence.

Finding Purpose and Meaning

It's natural to reflect on the deeper purpose and meaning of our existence. We may ask ourselves questions like, "Why am I here?" or "What is my purpose in life?" These are big questions, but seeking answers to them can be a powerful driver for personal growth and fulfillment. To find purpose and meaning, we may need to look beyond ourselves and consider our connection to the world around us. It's important to take stock of our values and beliefs and consider how they align with our actions and the impact we have on others. We can reflect on our strengths, passions, and talents, and consider how we can use them to contribute to something greater than ourselves.

Sometimes, finding purpose and meaning can involve taking risks and stepping outside of our comfort zones. It may require us to let go of limiting beliefs and self-doubt and embrace the unknown with an open mind and heart. It can be a journey of self-discovery and exploration, and it may take time and patience to uncover the answers we seek. However, as we cultivate gratitude and joy, and overcome obstacles and challenges, we may find that our purpose and meaning become clearer. We may discover that our journey of awakened consciousness is not just about our own personal growth and transformation, but also about serving a greater purpose and contributing to the wellbeing of others and the world around us. Ultimately, finding purpose and meaning is a lifelong journey, and one that can continue to evolve and unfold as we grow and learn. By staying connected to our inner selves, our intentions, and our values, we can continue to navigate this journey with authenticity and purpose and create a life that is rich with meaning and fulfillment.

It's easy to get lost in the day-to-day tasks of life and lose sight of the bigger picture. That's why finding purpose and meaning is so crucial to living a fulfilled life. It gives us a sense of direction and helps us prioritize our time and energy. One way to find purpose and meaning is to consider what brings you the most joy and fulfillment. Maybe it's spending time with loved ones, creating art, volunteering, or pursuing a specific career. Whatever it is, make sure it aligns with your values and beliefs. Another way to find purpose and meaning is to look for opportunities to make a positive impact on the world around you. This could be as simple as spreading kindness and positivity, or it could involve volunteering with a local organization or pursuing a career in a field that allows you to make a difference.

Whatever path you choose, remember that finding purpose and meaning is a passage, not an end point. Be open to new experiences and stay true to yourself, and you'll be on your way to living a life of purpose and meaning.

Navigating Relationships with Presence and Love

It's important to consider the role of relationships in our lives. Relationships can be a source of deep fulfillment and joy, but they can also bring challenges and difficulties that can be overwhelming. One key to navigating relationships with presence and love is to cultivate mindfulness in our interactions with others. This means being fully present and engaged in the moment, listening actively to what others are saying, and approaching each interaction with an open and compassionate heart. Another important aspect of navigating relationships is to practice empathy and compassion towards others. This means recognizing that everyone is struggling in their own way and seeking to understand their perspectives and experiences. By practicing empathy, we can deepen our connections with others and foster greater understanding and compassion in our relationships.

Finally, it's important to set healthy boundaries in our relationships, to ensure that we are taking care of our own needs and not sacrificing our well-being for the sake of others. This can involve learning to say "no" when necessary, communicating our needs clearly and assertively, and being willing to seek support when we need it. By approaching our relationships with presence, love, and compassion, we can deepen our connections with others and create a more fulfilling and joyful life.

Another way to cultivate an awakened consciousness is by navigating relationships with presence and love. This involves being fully present with our loved ones, listening with an open heart, and approaching conflicts with empathy and understanding. One way to practice this is by using active listening techniques. This involves giving our full attention to the person speaking, without interrupting or judging them. We can also practice empathy by trying to understand the other person's perspective, even if we don't agree with it.

Another important aspect of navigating relationships with presence and love is setting healthy boundaries. This means being clear about our own needs and limitations and communicating them respectfully to others. When we respect our own boundaries, we teach others to do the same. Ultimately, the key to navigating relationships with presence and love is to approach them with a mindset of compassion and understanding. When we prioritize love and connection over being right or winning, we create the space for deeper and more fulfilling relationships.

Honoring the Sacred in Everyday Life

Honoring the Sacred in Everyday Life is about recognizing the beauty and significance of every moment. We don't need to go to a mountaintop or a temple to experience the sacred; it is present in our everyday lives if we only take the time to notice it. One way to honor the sacred is through mindfulness. By being fully present in the moment, we can appreciate the beauty and wonder of our surroundings, whether it be the warmth of the sun on our skin or the sound of birds singing in the morning. We can also bring mindfulness to our daily activities, such as eating, walking, or even washing dishes. Another way to honor the sacred is by living in alignment with our values and principles. When we act with integrity and compassion, we are living in harmony with the sacred within ourselves and in the world around us. We can also honor the sacred by being kind to others and by showing gratitude for the blessings in our lives.

We can honor the sacred by cultivating a sense of reverence and awe for the mysteries of existence. Whether it be contemplating the vastness of the universe or the intricacy of a flower, we can recognize the beauty and wonder of creation and feel a deep sense of connection to something greater than ourselves.

Honoring the sacred in everyday life involves recognizing the interconnectedness of all things and treating everything with reverence and respect. This includes the natural world, other people, and even the small details of our daily routines. One way to honor the sacred in everyday life is to cultivate a sense of gratitude and appreciation for everything around us. This can be as simple as taking a moment to pause and reflect on the beauty of a sunset or expressing gratitude for the food on our plate before a meal. Another way to honor the sacred is to practice mindfulness in our daily activities. By being fully present and engaged in the moment, we can appreciate the richness and depth of our experiences and find meaning in even the most mundane tasks.

Additionally, we can honor the sacred by living in alignment with our values and principles. This involves making conscious choices that reflect our deepest beliefs and commitments and acting in service of our highest aspirations. Ultimately, honoring the sacred in everyday life is about recognizing the inherent worth and dignity of all beings and treating them accordingly. By living in a way that reflects this understanding, we can cultivate a deep sense of connection and meaning in our lives.

Integrating Spirituality and Practicality

Integrating spirituality into our practical, everyday lives can be a challenge. It's easy to feel disconnected from our spiritual practices when we're caught up in the demands of work, family, and other responsibilities. However, we can find ways to infuse spirituality into our daily routines, no matter how busy we are. One way to do this is to make a conscious effort to bring awareness and intention to our daily activities. For example, we can approach our work with a sense of mindfulness and focus, or we can take time to appreciate the beauty of nature during our daily commute. By bringing a sense of presence and gratitude to our everyday experiences, we can begin to see the sacredness in even the most mundane aspects of our lives.

Another way to integrate spirituality into our practical lives is to find ways to give back to our communities and the world at large. This can be through volunteer work, activism, or simply being kind and compassionate to those around us. By living in service to others, we can tap into a deeper sense of purpose and connection with the world around us. Ultimately, integrating spirituality and practicality requires a willingness to see the interconnectedness of all things and to approach our daily lives with a sense of mindfulness and purpose. It may take time and practice, but with patience and dedication, we can cultivate a more meaningful and fulfilling existence.

Integrating spirituality and practicality involves finding ways to apply our spiritual beliefs and practices in our daily lives. This means taking the insights and awareness we gain from our spiritual practices and bringing them into our interactions with others, our work, and our daily routines. One way to do this is to set intentions for how we want to show up in the world and then take action to align our behavior with those intentions. For example, if we want to cultivate more compassion in our relationships, we can set the intention to actively listen to others and practice empathy. Another way to integrate spirituality and practicality is to infuse meaning into our daily activities. This can involve approaching even mundane tasks with a sense of presence and intentionality, such as bringing mindfulness to washing dishes or folding laundry. Ultimately, the key to integrating spirituality and practicality is to see them not as separate domains, but as interconnected aspects of our lives. By bringing our spiritual insights into our daily lives, we can create a more holistic and fulfilling way of being.

Embodying Awakened Consciousness in the World

Embodying awakened consciousness in the world is about taking the lessons and insights we've gained on our transcendence and applying them to our daily lives. It means living with greater awareness, compassion, and purpose, and using our newfound understanding to create positive change in our reality. One way to embody awakened consciousness is to act towards causes we care about. This can involve volunteering, donating to charity, or advocating for social and environmental issues. By acting in alignment with our values, we can make a tangible difference in the world and feel a sense of fulfillment and purpose. Another way to embody awakened consciousness is to lead by example in our personal and professional relationships. We can strive to communicate with honesty and compassion, to listen with an open mind, and to treat others with kindness and respect. By embodying these qualities, we can inspire others to do the same and create a ripple effect of positive change. Ultimately, embodying awakened consciousness is about living with intention and aligning our actions with our values. By doing so, we can create a more compassionate, just, and sustainable world for ourselves and future generations.

Reflection

As we reach the end of this journey, it is important to reflect on what we have learned and how we have transformed. Through our experiences of transcendence, we have awakened to a deeper understanding of ourselves and the world around us. We have let go of limiting beliefs and embraced new perspectives that have opened us up to endless possibilities.

Transformation is not an easy process, and it requires dedication and courage to take the steps necessary to achieve it. But as we have seen throughout this journey, the rewards of transformation are immeasurable. We have tapped into a greater sense of purpose and meaning in our lives and have found a sense of fulfillment that goes beyond material success.

The process of transcendence and transformation is ongoing. It is not something that we achieve once and then move on from. Rather, it is a continual process of growth and evolution that requires us to remain open to new experiences and perspectives. It is through this ongoing process that we continue to expand our understanding of ourselves and the world around us.

As we close this chapter of our journey, let us remember that we have the power to shape our own lives and the world around us. Let us continue to embrace the process of transformation, and to live our lives with purpose and intention. Let us remain open to the limitless possibilities that await us as we continue to journey towards becoming our best selves.